MYTH AND ME

MYTH AND ME

The Indian Story

Lakshmi Lal

Rupa & Co

Published 2003 by
Rupa & Co
7/16, Ansari Road, Daryaganj,
New Delhi 110 002

Sales Centres:

Allahabad Bangalore Chandigarh Chennai
Dehradun Hyderabad Jaipur Kathmandu
Kolkata Ludhiana Mumbai Pune

ISBN 81-7167-749-5

Typeset in 11 pts. Memoir by
Nikita Overseas Pvt Ltd,
1410 Chiranjiv Tower,
43 Nehru Place
New Delhi 110 019

Printed in India by
Rekha Printers Pvt. Ltd,
A-102/1 Okhla Industrial Area, Phase-II,
New Delhi-110 020

To
acchan and amma
my enduring myths

and
acknowledging with reverence
my teacher
Professor G.H. Godbole of Mumbai

Tamil verses
selected by Valli Nagappan
rendered into English by Lakshmi Lal

Illustrations:
author's collection of Badri Narayan drawings

Contents

The Story Spreads   127

Preface

You are my wisdom, my dharma, the core of my being
you are the pride in my strength, the love in my heart
the form and beauty of all our gods
in all our temples throughout the land
come alive for you, are yours.

—Subrahmanya Bharati
(on Mother India)

Much of my youth was spent in being resolutely Indian. Resolutely, because it was not easy. The sun had not quite set on the British Empire and we still lived in its rosy afterglow.

My mother gave me a headstart. She coloured my dreams with readings from Kalidasa, Bhartruhari and Adishankara in her rich and ringing voice. She read, recited, chanted, intoned and explained passages from the *Upanishads*, particularly the *Kathopanishad* and interspersed it with Shankara's *Bhashyas* and *Stotras*.

It was a heady mix. Kalidasa remains to this day the highwater mark of the romantic imagination for me. Love in the rarified environs of Kubera's regions or on the snowbound heights of Shiva's Kailasa seemed well within human reach. Bhartruhari's *shatakas* (hundreds), three sets of a hundred verses each on erotica, politics and withdrawal ties up with the three stages of life following the initial seclusion of the student stage. It was an ideal introduction to the way the Hindu worries an idea to shreds and then tidies it all up into neat categories. Nachiketa's dialogues with death in the *Kathopanishad*, the logic of *karma* and re-birth made a deep and lasting impression; and Shankara became a model, almost without equal, for the pursuit of the spirit through the intellect, the *jnana marga* or the way of self-knowledge through enquiry. The Upanishadic seers were visionaries who questioned their way through the mere facts of life to the truth that lies beyond. And they were master raconteurs whose tales of adventures in the realms of the spirit one could not easily dismiss. I never looked back.

India has been called the story-teller of the world. Besides the *Ramayana* and the *Mahabharata* we have the *Jatakas*, the *Panchatantra*, the *Hitopadesha*, the *Vetala Panchavimshati* and the *Puranas*, to name only the better known collections. The story is the great Indian pastime. This applies equally to history. Facts become story becomes legend and soon enough a myth is born. With myths enter insights pointing to the truth that lies veiled and out of sight. Myths are pathways to Truth, shorn of mystique and accessible to all. The fact of Rama or Krishna, if and when they ever existed, is not nearly as relevant as the powerful myths they generated.

Myth, legend and folklore have also been a prime cultural and educational tool in India. Our fine and performing arts, whether of street, village, court or temple, throughout the country draw heavily upon them. They form a common resource pool for this vast nation with its maddening diversity. They gather this diversity and lead it to some sort of unity. As far as India goes, sufficient unto eternity is the myth thereof. Our story-hoard is truly inexhaustible. Illiteracy in India has not been quite the disaster it might have been because the village story-teller and all our arts, our rituals and our festivals have spread wide the wisdom encapsulated in our myths.

In western cultures the whole concept has been devalued along with the word. A myth is something to be exploded. The Indian tradition advises us to pay serious attention to a myth, reflect upon it, make it part of our lives and wait patiently for its meaning to dawn upon our consciousness with maturity and experience. For the meaning of an enduring myth might well be part of the meaning of life itself.

We could choose to spend our lives exploding myths or examining them. I fervently hope that East remains East and West remains West if in the meeting of the twain our myths explode and go up in a puff of global smoke.

The Indian is myth-born and myth-fed. We must consciously preserve this tradition now that the world is truly upon us with the endless allure of what money can buy. In going global with Bacardi rum, Coca-Cola, free sex and instant gratification we must not lose sight of the rich and continuing culture that is India. It would indeed be a pity if a commercially projected lifestyle based on purely materialistic sights wiped out the values put painstakingly together by an ancient civilisation such as ours.

India stimulates and excites me; and it never fails to amaze me. The wonder that is India helps me also to absorb the shock that India can frequently be. Five thousand years of vintage wisdom garnered by a long line of outstanding seekers is no mean heritage. I choose not to ignore it.

I have lived India in my head for more years than I care to remember. It has proved to be a good way, for the Indian journey is nothing if not inward.

My book begins with a general survey of the Hindu-Indian world-view as it grew and took shape to influence the Indian consciousness. From this flow the contents— the gods, the myths, the legends and the way they have spread through the performing and other arts to contribute to the strong and distinct infusion that is Indian culture. Hinduism remains the mainstream religion of India and therefore forms the basis for my presentation of the myths of India. It is, as it were, the host to all the religions that came to take root and flourish here. And it has been in spite of contemporary protests, a good and hospitable host.

Lakshmi Lal

THE STORY BEGINS

...... with the Vedas. The Vedas go the way of
intuition, insight, vision, transcendence. It is the
path of revelation that our seers and sages trod—
inwards into the caverns of their minds, the
spaces of their hearts. They mirrored and
communicated what they perceived in flashes as
the core of their being—and ours. It is this that
grows and branches out over time as a pantheon
with its accompanying myths and legends.

Long live the reciters of Vedas, our gods and our cattle
let rains drench the earth, and rulers stand tall
may all bad things be wiped out quite
as Hara's name sounds through the land
and the whole wide world be cleansed.

— Gnanasambandar

The Hindu-Indian World-View

A blade of grass, a shrub, a worm, a tree
animals, too, of many kinds; bird and snake
as man, as spirit, as heavenly gnome
demon and sage, the gods themselves
worlds animate and inanimate I've traversed
through birth after birth after birth
now, spent and quite worn out, my Lord
I see your precious golden feet and know
I'm home at last.

— Manikkavachakar

Religion is a way of looking at life with the sole purpose of working it out. The Hindu not only looks at life but stares at it, outstares it in fact till life is obliged to step aside and stop blocking the view. Then the veil of illusion lifts, the cloud of unknowing parts and Truth stands revealed; or rather realized. This is the way the Hindu sees it.

Hinduism is the mainstream religion of India, where it took root and flourished. At the end of a series of migrations from other lands, the Aryan influx took place. It was a significant entry. The Aryans infiltrated, as well as absorbed, the already indigenous inputs of the Austrics and the Dravidians. It was this Aryan chemistry that fashioned to a large extent what we now identify as Hinduism. This was the Vedic period, assumed to be around 1500 B.C. or so. The Aryan influx theory has been questioned. It is held by some that the Aryans were inhabitants of India and that the Vedas were revealed to them on the banks of the river Sindhu.

Hinduism, therefore, goes back to primitive and primordial beliefs that interacted with the simple nature worship of the Aryans who used the sacrificial fire to mediate between Heaven and Earth. The Vedas are intuitions, insights, visions of enlightened seeker-sages and also a compendium, a system of ritual sacrifices to be performed for the fulfilment, mainly, of worldly desires. This includes, of course, a place in Heaven. They consist of chants and hymns, sacred formulae, poems, songs and various rites. All this material was grouped into four *samhitas* or collections—*Rig Veda, Yajur Veda, Sama Veda* and *Atharva Veda*. Elemental forces were personified and deified. To name a few— Indra was the chief of the gods, Vayu the wind god, Varuna, god of the skies, Mitra, a solar deity and Agni, god of fire. Agni held the very special position of linking heaven and earth by carrying the sacrificer's plea to the gods. It was a young and simple world-view, the vision of nomadic settlers and agriculturists, shining with new-found optimism. It also had a deep sense of awe and mystery, as is clear from the literature that grew around the Vedas—the Brahmanas and the Aranyakas. These were really workshops and seminars on Vedic ritual and practice and proved to be fertile ground for the age of questioning that followed, the era of the Upanishads, extending roughly from 1200 B.C.—600 B.C. Some two hundred Upanishads have survived; of these 108 are considered important and twelve or thirteen, major and dominating. The Upanishads are sometimes referred to as Vedanta—end or culmination of the Vedas. 'Upanishad' could be interpreted as sitting next to, being near, which is the traditional Indian learning posture. One learns as much by proximity and absorption as by instruction.

Understandably, people realized that there was more to life than ritual and sacrifice. And this process was hastened by the stranglehold that the priests and the ritualists began to have on the lay Hindu. They had power and authority but not the answers. The Upanishads which are tracts, treatises and dialogues, conceptualised human experience into visions of Truth. Facts and Reality are stepping stones, and Truth, to cut a long, involved and at times nonsensical story short, is *Brahman*, the Supreme who is One, Indivisible and All-Pervading and who is to be tracked down in the spaces of each one's innermost, secret recesses. In fact, one school of thought, *Advaita* (non-duality) led by Shankara, the great ninth-century philosopher, goes something like this: "We are, each one of us, Brahman, for Brahman is all there is: only we don't know it, till we know it."

Brahman is a concept hard to pin down because it is beyond logic and certainly beyond words. "That from which words turn back, not having reached", is one sage's definition. But that of course did not stop the scholars and seers from beating about the Brahman bush for centuries. All sorts of things came flying out at them, concepts and ideas which proved to be invaluable aids in their quest. They recorded these and realized while doing so that Truth, now firmly identified with Brahman could only be approached through riddle and paradox. Life was not a tidy bed of consistencies. It was full of loose and flying ends. But then, the way to sense has often lain through non-sense.

Brahman is an abstraction to end all abstractions. It was the singlemost important discovery of the Upanishadic period. With it everything seemed to come together. It became not only the basis of Hinduism, but the unifying and binding factor in a religion that was so diverse and varying in its beliefs and rituals, so divided by history and geography, so tolerant of even new and deviant cults, that it could have splintered into non-existence. All roads and all schools of thought seemed to lead to Brahman, just as all numbers fell into place with the discovery of *shunya*, the zero. *Shunya,* or nothing was also everything.

Around this time there also arose—it is hard to phrase that in any other way—the two great epics, the *Ramayana* and the *Mahabharata*, both of which included, extended and spread the message of all the soul-searching that had gone on. They brought it down and out into the open and spread it far and wide—as did poetry, song, dance and theatre in the centuries that followed. It is the great Hindu achievement. All those findings would have died a natural death in their excluding and exclusive circles if myth, legend and story had not soaked them up for general consumption.

First impressions might lead one to believe that the Upanishadic seers moved in a rarified atmosphere of spiritual wool-gathering. This is not so. The atmosphere is electric rather than ethereal and crackles with the excitement of journeys into unknown and uncharted realms. I look upon the Upanishads as travellers' tales full of the thrill of discovery, crafted with care and designed to hold a wondering audience spellbound. Their magic is the magic of the concrete, the tangible, the homely for their aim was to relate the wanderings of the spirit and the intellect to everyday realities, to the mundane and the humdrum. The teachings are profound but the settings are familiar, everyday scenes.

We come next to the concretisation of the great abstraction, Brahman, the idea of an imaged God to be worshipped which gradually evolved and took over the task of preserving this way of life called Hinduism. Concepts of creation, preservation and destruction were shaped into the Hindu triad—Brahma, Vishnu and Shiva.

These then embraced or espoused their respective female counterparts, their powers, their *shaktis*. Brahma, the Creator acquired Saraswati, goddess of speech, learning and wisdom. She sprang from his side. Vishnu, the Preserver found Lakshmi who emerged full-blown from the mythical ocean of milk—it was a case of love at first sight. Shiva, the Destroyer consorted with Parvati, daughter of the Himalayas. She was the epitome of divine domesticity. In this case it was flight at first sight. Shiva fled at the thought of a possible involvement with Parvati because he was also the archetypal yogi. He was wooed by her and eventually won over.

The pantheon began to grow and proliferate. More and more concepts needed to be housed in concrete forms. Brahma receded into a mere creative backdrop, hardly imaged in the sanctum, and barely worshipped. Vishnu had ten incarnations, some growing into great and independent gods like Rama and Krishna. Shiva had two unique progeny. The elder, Ganesha, materialised as Parvati scrubbed herself while bathing. The younger, Kumara, was borne by Ganga, Parvati's sister and nurtured by the Pleiades. Durga, a more powerful associate form of Parvati, a collective fusion of the strength of all the gods and bearing all their weapons, came riding on a charging lion out of the Vindhyas. She was summoned into existence to banish evil in the form of a buffalo demon, Mahishasura. She has even more blood-thirsty and terrible offshoots—Kali and Chandi. These and many more have their regional, provincial or village variations. Their genealogies and histories are recorded in the *puranas* (ancient lore) and *sthalapuranas* (temple-site chronicles), a body of literature that came into existence in the early years after Christ, when also *bhakti* or unswerving devotion to a chosen deity became the Indian answer to all ills. People grew fiercely possessive of their gods, selected with great care by village, family and individual. The concept of a chosen god, *ishtadevata,* to whom an individual or group is drawn by habit, instinct, unreasoning attraction or even wild desire, is a unique Hindu concept. It is a highly personalised approach to worship and allows for a warmth and intimacy that takes the fear and foreboding out of divinity as defined by most religions. The Hindu can choose his god, then change his mind and choose all over again till he finds what suits him, with no blame attaching. Even gods are subject to review and life-long scrutiny.

As is clear by now, the word 'God' connotes differently in the Hindu vision. For one thing, he is not God Almighty. Gods, like all creation, belong to the secondary sphere—of manifestation or *maya,* in the cosmic scheme. However, they serve as necessary steps to Truth or Brahman. We must hold on to the concrete before we let go for the great leap forward into total abstraction. And that leap is inwards, as we have seen, into 'the space within our hearts,' the *hridayi akasha,* the metaphysical term for this space.

The following are a few key concepts that unlock the Hindu mystique and shed light on this way of life called Hinduism.

Varnashrama Dharma

This is the dual track on which a Hindu's life on earth runs—*varna* (caste) and *ashrama* (one's stage in life). There are four castes: the intellectual and the priestly *(brahmin)*, the martial and the kingly *(kshatriya)*, the merchant and the trader *(vaishya)* the menial and the worker *(shudra)*. Caste divisions were not wholly rigid. Upward mobility was in-built to some extent. There are four ashramas or stages in an individual's life-cycle: *brahmacharya* (student), *grihasta* (householder), *vanaprastha* (retirement), *sannyasa* (withdrawal).

These are the societal parameters within which a Hindu operates. *Varna*, caste, is breaking up but like most things in India, very gradually. The ashrama still remains the Hindu ideal. You let go in the end but not of your Self. You only retreat to focus on the inner life.

Dharma is a term that cannot be translated, only freely rendered. I would venture a definition on the following lines: a rule of law and conduct tailored to your role in society and also your personality. *Swadharma*, your very own niche or role in life and *swabhava*, your very own nature or personality are areas for each one to explore, discover and be true to. It is in that sense that *dharma* becomes a duty and a responsibility, primarily to yourself as a member of society.

The four aims of life are *dharma, artha, kama, moksha. Dharma* is a life-long companion, and the foundations are laid early, as a student or *brahmachari*. It is the steady undercurrent on which you are borne and kept afloat. It helps you to navigate the turbulent waters of life. *Artha* is the pursuit of worldly wealth. Kama is the pursuit of sensuous and sexual pleasures. Artha and kama are the legitimate pre-occupations of the *grihasta,* the householder. *Moksha* should be the pre-occupation of the last two stages of life, a goal attained by most only over many life-times. The idea is to cut loose or obtain *mukti* from the cycle of births and deaths, achieve release from human bondage and realize the oneness of pure being. Detachment and limited involvement in all activity are the exercises prescribed for this final aim.

Gunas are the three proclivities or ingredients which permeate all creation, both animate and inanimate. Each one of us, including the gods, is subject to this mix, with one or the other predominating. Brahma is *rajas,* representing activity, Creation. Shiva is *tamas,* representing Destruction leading to inertia, inaction. Vishnu is *sattva,* representing Preservation, maintenance. All three *gunas* dissolve into perfect balance and equilibrium, nullifying each other in the state of non-manifestation, *Brahman.* Brahman thus becomes *nirguna,* devoid of guna or attribute. Gunas have wide-ranging applications. They tie up with temperament, personality, aura, mood, colour, even food. Sattva is white, rajas red and tamas black, brown or dark. The sattvic mood is bright and still, the rajasic restless, excitable and active, the tamasic dark, heavy, brooding. Sattvic food is bland, austere, pure. It is appropriate for brahmins, nourishing the intellect. Rajasic food is appetising, fiery, energising, food for men of action—kshatriyas and vaishyas, the warrior class and merchants. Tamasic food is heavy, filling, coarse—food fit and proper for manual labour and menials. For the practical, wider needs of societal functioning, the appropriate food for each class or caste has been identified and recommended. Parallel to all this run the aspirations of the individual who is questioning and questing at one level or another. Here, personality and its development comes into play as also free will and individual choice.

Applied to personality, the three gunas manifest themselves in varying proportions in each person. The sattvic personality is serene, tranquil. The rajasic is dynamic and on the move. The tamasic tends to be inert, brooding, phlegmatic with a hint of menace. We are expected to analyse, then distil our individual compositions and refine them till the sattvic predominates, for through the sattvic, one pursues moksha. It is the final filter. This is where yoga helps. Yoga cleanses and prepares us for good living in the truest sense, aiming at release which is, by Hindu standards, the only aim worth having.

Leela is sport, the play of life. In its divine context, it is the theatre of the gods. The stage is here on earth and gods sport partly to entertain themselves, but mainly to direct the attention of humanity to the veiled mystery that is life. We are drawn to the show by the tricks of *maya*, the stage effects. Every now and then the curtains part to provide a glimpse of what goes on behind the scenes. If we pursue it to see where it leads, we have begun the quest for Truth. Leela is meaningful play or learning through fun, call it what you may.

Maya is part of the cosmic game plan. One has to cope with it, contend with it, be part of it and ultimately see through it. Maya is golden and radiant, it dazzles and blinds. In the *Ishopanishad* there is reference to a hymn, the hymn of a dying man to the sun, the source of all life. He makes a moving plea, asking the sun to move aside so that he can look at the bare truth. It is the most telling image of *maya* that I have come across.

Life, Time and Circumstance

No discussion of the Hindu world-view is complete without outlining the Hindu concepts of life, time and circumstance. Time and life belong to mortality. What is born has to die with the passage of time, usually accumulating circumstance (*karma*) through action, with Fate or Destiny standing by.

Most religions are agreed on this and each one deals in its own way with a life after death, giving that life a spot in heaven or hell, or variations thereof. The Hindu too has a heaven and a hell; or rather many heavens and hells but they are temporary, inhabited by gods and anti-gods; and we have already seen that the gods are not almighty or all-powerful, nor even sufficient unto themselves. Heaven and hell are karmic traps and need to be worked out of our systems.

The human goal for a Hindu is not a place but a state of mind, a state of consciousness, release or *moksha*. What binds or tethers is karma. Karma is the cause that produces the effect called life. To live is to act, to act is to generate *karma* which then leads to repeated births and deaths. The secret is to act without involvement, to disengage oneself. Then, and only then can the vicious cycle of birth and death be cut. This is the central lesson of the *Bhagavad Gita*, Krishna's advice to Arjuna on the battlefield of Kurukshetra.

Applied to creation, time passes in larger circles. The dawn of creation launches a *yuga* or age of innocence, the Sata Yuga. This is followed by a less glorious, but still good period, the Treta Yuga. Then comes a mixed yuga of vice, virtue and confusion, the Dwapara Yuga. Lastly, just before the final dissolution, comes the Kali Yuga, the point of no return. The cycle is complete, chaos reigns. The primal waters take over, a becalmed sea of inactivity, till the first ripple of movement bursts into another cycle of time and creation, another Mahayuga comprising yet another series of four yugas.

Around this core are many creation myths. The point to note is that nothing is final, not even doomsday. All is flux, time is endless, life is a bore and a scare even for the Creator, which is why he creates in the first place. What frequently seems like apathy, resignation, fatalism is just acknowledgement and acceptance of this fact. What appears to be indifference or lack of motivation could well be an unconscious exercise in transcendence, the Hindu's unique motivation. The Hindu strives like anyone, anywhere but deep inside, he or she is striving not for this life or even a life hereafter but cessation, leading to *sat* or 'being', synonymous with essence. It is the Hindu strength and failing.

Sound as Mantra

A good mind needs to chant no mantra
nor to raise and hold its breath
no yogic feats need it perform
mantras thrive in minds prepared.

— Tirumoolar

There is an ancient Indian dream. It is a dream of Fact and Reality from which you wake to Truth. All Hindus are born with it. They seek to find it in lives past, present or to come. For in dreaming it we fulfil ourselves; it is the Hindu dream of dreams.

Rishis, munis and sannyasis are possessed and propelled by it. Their minds, crazed by its mystery, grasp it through the white heat of their blazing intellects. The still waters of their hearts reflect it as a mountain lake images the sky or as a crystal holds the clairvoyant's gaze.

They follow it to the ends of worlds known and unknown, and to their own inner voids. There, in echoing, mystic spaces, the caverns of the mind, its chasms, they hear the truth and perceive it, rather than understand it.

Seers have tried to speak of their vision, to articulate it. But the truth is unspeakable. At best it can only be uttered. Each such utterance becomes a 'sound' of truth, offered up as an act of worship, in a state of contemplation and deep meditation. And a formula of spiritual refuge, charged with the force of insight, a thought-form, a mantra is born.

That is what mantra is all about—sound as incantation, formulated to vibrate its way to truth. The Vedas, the Puranas and all our greatest hymns of praise enshrine this philosophy, a philosophy of sound, patterned to capture the Illusive Reality, and through it, the Abiding Truth. Words and their meanings, language and its associations can and do figure in a mantra, but the essence of it is an almighty babble. Truth, to draw a Christian parallel, is something that issues "out of the mouths of babes"—and babes can only babble. So did the Delphic oracles. So did our seers.

The early revealed knowledge of the Hindus, the Vedas, in their most inspired and valued sections, are a babble of mantras heard by the inner ear of illumined souls. They are recited, chanted or sung in simple or elaborate metres, in endless permutations and combinations that include every conceivable variable of time, space and circumstance. The sound of truth is, of necessity, complex. For it has to confront the complexity of time, life and death, before overpowering and progressing beyond it. Seventy million main mantras are believed to exist, besides countless secondary ones. They cover all probable and possible exigencies of body, mind and soul in their troubled path through life after death after life, in the turning giant-wheel of re-birth. Before one goes on to examine some main mantras and their areas of influence, it might be well to explore for a bit the concept of sound in the Hindu scheme of spirituality.

Creation centres on sound and its chief application, speech. An eighteenth-century saint-musician, Kalidas Paramahans, has expressed it beautifully—"The Creator wakes and OM is manifest—the core of Being, primeval resonance".

The stuff of which the world is born is vibration, and its concomitant, sound. The *shakti* or female energy of Brahma, the Creator, is *Vak,* or speech, deified as Saraswati. In the beginning, indeed, was the word. It is by sounding the depths of primeval inertia that worlds spin into existence. Nadabrahman, the Creator as sound, resonates before his will to create achieves materialisation. *OM*, sound of sounds, is nothing but the hum of creation.

Once sound is identified as the hinge upon which all creation swings into being, it is easy to grasp the mysterious power of mantras, the sounds of truth. Each mantra, in practice, is an act of worship directed towards a specific deity. The system of mantras, therefore, becomes a system of deities, invoked for communion with Truth, and vividly visualised.

All this is not to say that *mantra* belongs only to the realm of rarified consciousness, that it ignores the Reality of here-and-now. Mantra has a practical, pragmatic aspect which its occult and mystic elements might mask. The way to Truth lies through Reality, and only through Reality. Once you are born, life is inescapable. And there is only one thing you can do with it—live it. Preferably fully, and to the best of your ability. Mantra is a scheme for successful living.

Modern psychology aims at well-adjusted, fully developed personalities and concerns itself with the process of self-development. So does mantra. The aim of psychology and mantra are the same—up to a point and with one difference. The modern science of psychology limits itself to this world. The ancient science of mantra goes beyond it. Self-development leads to self-realization: to realize one's self is to arrive at the Abiding Truth. All the rest is only preparation for this, not an end in itself.

Even the methods of psychology and mantra are the same—guidance, counselling and treatment. This is where a guru comes in. Finding a suitable mantra is no easy job. It has to fit the personality, the circumstances, the individual's stage of development. A mantra must be custom-chosen, prescribed by a professional with experience and knowledge, in other words, a guru.

Most mantras also have an immediate, worldly purpose. There are mantras, for instance, to conquer sleep, to create fire, to extinguish fire, to acquire powers of levitation, even to destroy enemies.

Sir John Woodroffe, writing as Arthur Avalon, sums up a mantra as "power (shakti) in the form of sound". The power of a mantra is, in actuality, the power generated by a fully-flowered personality, functioning under its influence and by its proper practice. The magic of mantra, in that sense, is no different from the magic of a successful, confident personality, fulfilling itself.

Like root-words in language, there are *bija* or seed mantras. These are highly condensed, mono-syllabic codes that, properly recited, after due initiation by a guru or preceptor, release immeasurable powers in the contemplating soul. At the head of this list stands the all-inclusive, universal mantric formula, the mystic OM or AUM. This syllable, according to one Upanishad is composed of eight subtle sound elements—A, U, M, the nasalisation, the sound, the duration, its resonance within time, and lastly, its timeless resonance. The *Mandukya Upanishad* gives it prime place in the scheme of things: "AUM. This syllable is the whole world. It is the past, the present, the future. Everything is just the word AUM. And whatever else there is ... that, too, is just the word AUM".

AUM is considered by some to be a compendium of the three members of the Hindu triad. 'A' stands for Brahma and the evolving tendency, *rajas*, wakefulness, action. 'U' stands for Vishnu, the tendency to cohesion, *sattva*, the state of dream, the power of thought. 'M' represents Shiva and the powers of darkness and disintegration, the *tamas* tendency, the state of deep sleep and the power of consciousness. It also stands for the one unchanging being pervading space, time and form.

We see therefore, in AUM a whole religious and spiritual scheme, an entire cosmology. It is the code that, once broken, unlocks the universe and gives the devout a glimpse into its mystic recesses. All systems, be they Yogic, Vedic or Tantric, recognise and bow down to its significance. AUM, in the primeval language of mantras, means 'I assent, I accept'. And the humility of acceptance is the beginning of realization, of mukti. Other noteworthy bija mantras are AIM, dedicated to Saraswati, Goddess of Speech, leading to knowledge, wisdom, mastery over words; SHRIM, to Lakshmi, Goddess of Fortune and Prosperity, leading to power, beauty, glory, wealth.

Sometimes bija mantras are strung together into garlands of sound-power, such as the one to *Parashakti* (Supreme Energy). Sometimes, a verse or prayer with an external or exoteric meaning can be a powerful mantra. Among these, the *Gayatri*, a solar mantra stands supreme. Directed to the Sun, its twenty-four syllables scan to the Gayatri metre, a metre which in itself has been deified and visualised—so sacred is its measured grandeur supposed to be. It is this mantra which the brahmin receives when he dons the sacred thread and is pronounced twice-born, and which it then becomes his duty to recite during the three daily meditations—morning, noon and sunset.

The Gayatri was an exclusive preserve of the brahmins who, in the Hindu system of caste, were made to bear both the privileges and the burdens of all intellectual and spiritual pursuits. Its meaning, which deepens with meditation and contemplation into endless esoteric chasms is, simply translated: "AUM! O terrestrial sphere! O sphere of space! O celestial sphere! Let us contemplate the splendour of the solar spirit, the Divine Creator. May he guide our minds. AUM!"

There are legends about the power of the *Gayatri* in oral spiritual lore. A brahmin, Vidyaranya, had recited the Gayatri twenty-four lakh times with no effect. In his despondency he turned to a tantrik who promised him release and deliverance in ten days through dread rites performed in cemeteries to invoke Bhairavi, a terrifying aspect of Devi. The brahmin agreed to try the tantric method. It worked. At the end of the stipulated period, Bhairavi appeared but would not approach close enough for benediction. Nonplussed, Vidyaranya wanted to know the reason. The Devi replied that the power of his twenty-four lakh Gayatri repetitions would destroy her if she came any closer. Vidyaranya had learnt his lesson. Armed with this new-found wisdom, he returned to Vedic rites and with further repetitions of the Gayatri, he achieved moksha, liberation from the bondage of re-birth.

A powerful mantra like the *Gayatri*, incorrectly or half-heartedly uttered, can do harm. King Janaka, an ardent Gayatri follower, was a wise and devout King. One day, as he passed the royal stables, a baby elephant with the power of human speech drew his attention. On entering into a conversation with the elephant he discovered that a brahmin who used to frequent his court had been re-born as this elephant because, in his previous life, he had recited the Gayatri heedlessly and half-heartedly.

Mantras have very strictly laid down conditions and strongly recommended methods for their *japa* or repetition. The *Agni Purana* points out, for instance, that a mantra, softly spoken, is more effective than if repeated loudly; that repeated with lip movements only, it is a hundred times more potent and that mentally and inwardly repeated, its power increased a thousand-fold. Modern psychology which advocates soft-sell and recommends the gentler, more hidden arts of persuasion would agree with the wisdom of this procedure. After all, a mantra is designed to woo and win a deity, to arrive at an elusive truth. A low-key, subtle, soft and private approach is bound to be more effective than a loud, demanding, public clamour for the deity's attention. After all, one must remember that Hindu deities are human!

Mantras can come in alluring disguise. The 'Saundarya Lahari' (Ocean of Beauty), ascribed to Adi Shankara is an example. At the most apparent level it is a descriptive, rapturous hymn to Devi, full of extremely sensuous, almost tactile imagery. And yet the whole hymn has been decoded to read as an elaborate hand-book of Devi mantras with an appropriate *yantra*, a ritual diagram, for each stanza. Our seers spoke in riddles, and Shankara, the ninth-century founder of Advaita, nondualism, who dwarfs most intellects, master-minded this *mantric* puzzle as a multi-level spiritual experience. The opening stanza, according to one commentator, is open to fourteen different interpretations, depending on the approach taken! Such are the mazes of Indian philosophical and mystical literature.

Mantras cannot be self-taught. There is no do-it-yourself way to a mantra. It has to be given to you by a guru, a preceptor. Initiation is implicit in the mantric way of thinking. However industrious and learned a person, he cannot give himself a mantra. A seer, a rishi, a guru, a divine vision, an insight—he must wait for one of these to bless him with his mantra and this might involve years of patient waiting, futile search or even deception, as in the case of the great mystic, Kabir. Kabir, a humble weaver of Banaras, just could not get through to his guru. The learned man chose to ignore the devout Kabir's repeated attempts. Kabir found a way out. One day, in the darkness of pre-dawn, he lay on the steps of a holy ghat directly in the guru's path as he went down the steps to the water's edge. Stepping on Kabir, he involuntarily exclaimed 'Ram, Ram' in a spontaneous gesture of apology and passed on. Kabir guessed that it was the guru's personal mantra and, later, claimed that he had received it from the guru himself. The guru gracefully acknowledged Kabir's fitness to receive it.

Mantras are the wizardry of Indian truth. Their magical connotation extends, in certain cults and practices, to witchcraft, sorcery and exorcism; for magic can be both black and white. In fact, in the mantric context, there is a spectrum of five colours—white, gold, red, blue and black—symbolising various states of mind. Red is physical, blue spiritual, yellow intellectual, white stands for pure spirit, black for negation—hence the black arts. It is the colour of a personality that we recognise as his or her distinctive aura. Aura is a vital element in all worship and ritual. The mood of the worshippers is directed by it, or alternatively generates it. One cannot speak of Mantra without touching upon *Tantra* and *Yantra*. Tantra, which Philip Rawson describes as 'the Indian cult of ecstasy', relies heavily on *mantra*. It also harnesses female sexual power to uncoil, awaken and direct the 'serpent power', *kundalini,* to travel up the mystic spine, through six stages, in an ascent of 'release'. The symbolism of Tantra is sexual and its approach, sensuous and sensual, is one of joy not denial. To quote Rawson, Tantra urges you to "raise your enjoyment to its highest power, and then use it as a spiritual rocket-fuel".

Tantra also relies heavily on yantra. A yantra is a geometrical diagram which serves as an icon charged with symbolism. The key yantra of Tantrism is the Shri Yantra which is really a symbolic diagram of Genesis. It has a focal point, the *bindu,* a central dot which, with its first movement, gives rise to a female and then a male triangle. From this original couple, or more correctly, their coupling, the universe unfolds and takes shape.

Arthur Avalon in 'Serpent Power' gives us an excellent measure of the wide-ranging nature of this ancient Indian magic called mantra. It is an appropriate note to end on for there is a tendency to equate mantra with goodness and beneficence—the malevolence implicit in it, its dark and menacing aspects, are often missed out.

"There is nothing necessarily holy about a mantra. Mantra is a power (Mahashakti) which lends itself impartially to any use. A man may be killed or injured by mantra".

Magic is born of imagination: and imagination ranges freely over the entire landscape of man's consciousness. Mantra, which is nothing if not magic and wizardry, must therefore take in darkness as well as light, terror as well as joy, evil as well as good. The attempt of our seers is to bend mantra to productive, positive purposes; to avoid the destructive and the negative. Mantra is a double-edged sword. Used discerningly, it can clear the path to Truth. Handled carelessly, it can cut. Once acquired, it is a secret weapon that never fails the trained and skilled user. Or so the Hindus, and indeed the Buddhists and the Jains believe.

Purusha and Prakruti

Wisdom and Spirit of the Universe!
Thou Soul that art the Eternity of Thought!
That giv'st to forms and images a breath
And everlasting motion!......

— William Wordsworth

The Indian metaphysical tradition, ancient and impressive in its continuity and persistence leaves us two signposts to the vast unknown, the uncharted realms of the spirit—the Unmanifest and the Manifest. In between lies the shimmering twilit area, Prakruti and her source, Purusha.

Before going on to Prakruti let us deal briefly with the Unmanifest and then leave it firmly alone. I use the term 'leave alone' advisedly because the Unmanifest does not lend itself easily to comprehension, and not at all to articulation. Worldly, not to mention, wordly faculties however refined, honed, crafted fail us here. The Unmanifest can only be inferred, taken on faith—or experienced. You can *be* it, and once you *are* it you do get back, but not to tell the tale, because it is inexpressible. You are silenced. 'Let it be' is the customary spiritual instruction on this matter.

Truth, Reality and Fact are the words, however inadequate, that will be used hereafter to signify the Unmanifest, Prakruti/Purusha and the Manifest, respectively. Briefly defined **Truth** is full, filling, complete with no room for accommodating anything else—perfect unity as opposed to mere union. **Reality,** transcendent and imaging the Truth, is Purusha and Prakruti in union and One, with the potential for division, parturition. One, as opposed to Zero or *Shunya* which applies to Truth. **Fact** or the Manifest is divided, endlessly divisible, and therefore multiple, multifarious with names, forms and categories—nama-rupa-samsara, the universe, our world, life here and now—complicated, complex, various, variegated, riddled with paradox, fraught with opposites.

Prakruti is both manifestor and manifestation because once manifest she is within, inside each one of her manifestations; and without, outside as Manifestor. She is the potential for Becoming as opposed to Being, for multiplicity as opposed to unity. S.N. Das Gupta calls her 'the immense potentiality of the whole world.' The potentiality referred to is the potentiality for creativity. Being the source for creativity, giving birth to it, she is

the womb, therefore female and inevitably Mother—
Mother of Mothers, Mother of Manifestation, Mother of
the Universe.

And Mothers go with Fathers. Here Purusha enters
unavoidably. Purusha and Prakruti together form the
substratum of Manifestation but Purusha, the Male is
inert, detached and non-participating. His kama, his
desire to Manifest, to be many, impels Prakruti to realise
her potential and come into existence as his power, his
shakti, his energy. John Woodroffe writing as Arthur
Avalon puts it very well when he says "Power is power
both to be and to become." Purusha, at one remove from
the Unmanifest or Truth just is, and changeless. Prakruti
is active, creative, willing, doing and becoming. Purusha
and Prakruti therefore can be called Being and Becoming,
respectively. Prakruti has the power to emerge, BECOME,
and again, and yet again be re-absorbed, merged in her
source, Purusha—to BE.

In mythology Shiva and Parvati, correspond to this
idea. Shiva's power, shakti, is Parvati most eloquently
expressed in the Ardhanari concept. Purusha and
Prakruti cannot exist one without the other; 'as one as
word and meaning', according to Kalidasa in his
invocation in 'The Raghuvamsha', Meaning is the shakti
of the word.

The many terms for Prakruti map her meaning. The
most interesting is *maya*, the shakti that is concomitant
with creation. She is not just illusion, she is a power. In
the Vedas she is the power that enabled asuras to change
form, to disappear and appear at will with intent to

mislead and deceive. Later, this got converted to a more positive and productive power—the power to reveal and conceal. The world as maya is a place where we get glimpses of the Truth when maya lets the veil either flap or develop peepholes depending on how focussed we are. Alternatively, when we are caught up in externals, embroiled, the curtain or veil of illusion blocks out and conceals.

Maya is also *avidya*, literally speaking, ignorance. Again it is not just this. Ignorance bears the sense of 'not perceiving' 'unaware' not using our native skills to see beyond. Maya is to be experienced in all her colour and excitement, life is to be lived here and now while at the same time we strain after the away and beyond. This extending and stretching leads us to the Reality, the Transcendental which infuses and informs the projection that is maya.

This brings us to *leela*, the play of the world, its sport in time and space that teases, beguiles and bewilders. It is an interesting side-effect or show of maya 'the eternal play in which the self hides and seeks itself'. The object always is to get behind the curtain and into the wings. In that sense, maya is the challenge that keeps us on our toes, reaching out and up.

Prakruti is *bindu*, the dimensionless dot, the seed, the potentiality, her Manifestor aspect. The sprout, the product is Manifestation. She is also *prana*, life-breath. Although prana is considered to reflect Purusha as reality, Prakruti in assuming her function as life-force, becomes it.

She is *Aditi*, difficult-to-split, Mother of the Gods; that is, the Manifestor of the gods themselves. She is also *Sesha* the serpent-bed of Vishnu who contains within himself the remnant (sesha), the germ of new worlds to come—potentiality in other words.

Prakruti, dormant as Manifestor is all the energies, forces, powers collectively, awaiting the moment of manifestation, expression; expended yet never depleted, the forever enduring potential, potent and creative. As Manifestation she is a reflection in the mirror that is Purusha, or to use another traditional image, a painting on the canvas that is Purusha.

Prakruti in action as Manifestor comes with her bag of three gunas (proclivities, tendencies) sattva, rajas, tamas. Sattva is white, light, bright, still, poised. Rajas is red, restless, active, passionate. Tamas is dark, inert, lethargic, fearsome.

All things, not merely living beings, even the gods, are made up of those three in varying proportions that determine their distinctive personalities and identities. Depending on your role in life and of course your destiny you develop one or the other. In the caste structure the brahmin or the intellectual focusses on sattva, the kshatriya and the vaishya, warrior and trader, on rajas, and the worker, shudra, on tamas. All these have now become birth-rights to be misused.

These proportions or mixes are not fixed and immutable—the aim is to increase the sattvic component because white and light is closest to the colourless, abstract Being, Purusha, as opposed to Becoming or Prakruti/Maya/Avidya.

Prakruti is in everything, even a seemingly lifeless stone. Stones may not breathe but they respond to stimuli. Homo sapiens is the highest evolute.

Prakruti at her lightest, subtlest and most translucent is in the human species; she gets grosser, thicker and more opaque down the scale.

In myth and legend she manifests as the Mother Goddess—Devi, Durga, Saraswati, Lakshmi, the Saptamatrikas. She is to be loved, reverenced, prayed to for protection—and feared. In the Hindu pantheon she proliferates in all her range and diversity. In the shakti cult she is the Supreme One and subjugating Purusha, almost dispenses with him. Gender wars and awareness is not a new thing. Nothing is.

Prakruti uses visionaries, seers, poets to display her awesome reach, and behind it all, even as she merges into Purusha periodically, she looks back and smiles at us as we struggle, trapped in the splendours of her creation, to see beyond. Or so I imagine.

I conclude with two expressions of Prakruti and Purusha from an unlikely source—English poetry.

The first is a stirring vision of Prakruti as Transcendental Reality, a poet's moment of revelation. The experience stands suspended between the world of Fact and the world of Truth—an intense, intuitive perception of Prakruti at play, the leela and the maya of it all.

'Led by Her' (Prakruti, Nature) the poet rows towards a craggy ridge—'the horizon's utmost boundary', an elfin pinnace. And this is what follows:

"When, from behind that craggy steep till then
The horizon's bound, a huge peak, black and huge
As if with voluntary power instinct
Upreared its head ... with purpose of its own
And measured motion like a living thing
Strode after me ... but after I had seen
That spectacle, for many days my brain
Worked with a dim and undetermined sense
Of unknown modes of Being ... No familiar shapes
Remained, ... no colours of green fields;
But huge and mighty forms that do not live
Like living men, moved slowly through the mind
By day, and were a trouble to my dreams."

> extract from 'The Prelude'
> by William Wordsworth

The second is a succint statement by Gerard Manley Hopkins, a poet whose mystical approach to Nature is rendered even more significant by his religious fervour—Hopkins was a priest. The first part of the poem is an apt description of Prakruti—it ends with the lines:

"All things counter, original, spare, strange
All things fickle, freckled (who knows how?)
With swift, slow; sweet, sour; adazzle, dim;"
and then enters Purusha:
"He fathers forth whose beauty is past change:
Praise him."

> an extract from 'Pied Beauty'
> by Gerard Manley Hopkins

Brahma the Creator

The Creator in the Hindu pantheon has the most dubious and controversial of origins, the most chequered of divine pasts, the least impressive of service records. In fact, his is a failure story in the worldly sense. He has been superceded by the other two luminaries of the triad—Vishnu the Preserver and Shiva the Destroyer, whose divine careers overshadow the evolution of this relatively inert and somewhat undramatic member of the Hindu triad. While Brahma has forfeited the right to be worshipped by humanity—and thereby hangs a tale or two—the temple bells of India ring out in endless praise of Vishnu and Shiva. They have most certainly stolen the show. Theirs is a success story.

Perhaps this reflects the Hindu view of the manifest world—a riddle, a puzzle, a jigsaw with missing pieces, somewhat carelessly assembled and in any case only a temporary, if necessary, step in the unrelenting path to *moksha*, liberation. The *maya* of it all covers many a fault. The creator of *maya,* Brahma, is only playing around with the stuff of space-time reality as a child prodigy would play with plasticine or building blocks. For one of the legends about Brahma presents him as becoming intensely aware of his terrible aloneness and, with the heat and fervour of creative activity, he summons into existence Vak, Saraswati, the Goddess of Speech. One thing leads to another; they come together repeatedly in the first of all sublime matings, to conjure up from the unmanifest formless, the tableaux, the masques of manifest creation. Another legend reinforces the idea of divine self-entertainment. Brahma experiences a sudden and intense consciousness of himself as Individual and breaks away from the Formless into Form; the first fledgling to fly the parental nest. Thereafter, within this scheme, he operates with sublime nonchalance, the aloof and uninvolved spectator.

Brahma, the four-faced, bearded, aged God originated in the Golden Embryo, *Hiranyagarbha,* afloat on the primal, causal waters. From his four heads emerged the four Vedas, the summation of all knowledge. He is also conceived as *swayambhu,* self-created. As the consort of Saraswati who sprang from his own being, there is an element of moral censure that clings to him—hence the reluctance to worship him, says one tradition. Another tradition holds that he fell into disgrace for telling a lie. He even produced two false witnesses to corroborate the claim. He was set the task of travelling to the end of a giant *linga* by Shiva. Brahma claimed to have seen its tip, was caught out and condemned to eternal oblivion. There is only one temple consecrated to the worship of Brahma—in Pushkar, Ajmer.

Brahma himself is limited in space and time. The manifest, created world has a life-span—all illusions have. The great *maya* is no exception. And the *Mayin*, its creator, will also cease to exist though unnumbered human years will pass before he does. Hence one must touch upon the Brahma time-scale.

Each created world remains unaltered for one day of Brahma, a period of virtually unnumbered years. Also one thousand cycles of the four Yugas (each running into thousands of human years) make one day of Brahma. And Brahma's life lasts for a hundred Brahma years. The world is while Brahma wakes—it ceases to be when he retires with divine clockwork regularity to sleep every night. He wakes again to create another world and sleeps away that one too and so on. But the game must cease, the toys must be put away. The puzzle is worth solving only up to a point.

The passiveness of the act of creation, the withdrawal from the scene of action, the spectator-like role of the creator, perhaps the knowledge that tomorrow is another day and yet another world, answers most of man's questions and stills most of his doubts. Brahma has immense stretches of time and limitless expanses of space to create in and from. He will design and reject and design again, raise the curtain on a different scene everyday of his conscious life. To awaken to brand new world patterns, to seek ever-fresh fields and ever-new pastures is surely a grandiose and mind-blowing

Brahma the Creator

pastime, a pastime fit for the gods. In this process, there is something in it for everybody, all creatures who wear motley and strut the world's stage.

And here we come to the universality of experience, a universality which all religions have arrived at, but which the poets most of all, and perhaps most effectively of all, have expressed. To quote English poets who would rate as alien or foreign to Oriental tradition and conditioning—"Life like a dome of many-coloured glass/ Stains the white radiance of eternity" (Shelley). "All the world's a stage...." and man is a bundle "of sound and fury, signifying nothing." (Shakespeare).

The very essence of life is paradox—so is the essence of Brahma, its creator. Brahma is, so to say, forces, energies, opposites held in delicate, even precarious balance. To resolve these in one's mind is no easy matter. One is brought up short at every stage by the basic contradictions of human existence.

I sum up with a recapitulation of the Hindu theory of creation, destruction and re-creation in order to wrest some order out of the haze of guesswork and speculation, and to fix Brahma, the evasive God, in my own mind. As the forces of destruction swallow up one created world leaving only the darkness of cosmic emptiness, a few embers of future activity lie dormant. These residual, latent traces of activity leap into fresh existence and create new worlds, which once again move towards extinction. We are back again to square, formless, one.

Vishnu the Preserver

> It was Shri I saw at first
> then his dazzling face
> and gleaming gold, his discus fierce
> that ploughs through enemy lines in battlefields
> the conch, too, nestling in his hand
> I saw, indeed I did
> my lord of the hue of oceans deep.

— Bhutattalvar

Vishnu, the Preserver, is a concept that burst out of its cocoon in a progressive, expansive spreading of divine wings, back through aeons of time and forward through centuries of human worship. The *Vishnu Purana* hails him as "the mighty over all: he who is *Hiranyagarbha* (Brahma), *Hari* and *Shankara;* the Creator, Preserver and Destroyer of the world".

He assumed with the effortlessness of the successful, the attributes and responsibilities of his triad-mates, Brahma the Creator and Shiva the Destroyer, bestowing on them their individual identities for purely functional purposes with the grace of a truly supreme Godhead.

Vishnu usurps the causal waters, trespassing on creative territory and, in a superb gesture of good management has Brahma emerging at the start of each new world from his navel, seated on a resplendent golden lotus of a throne. And, presumably, through a visionary haze projects his *maya*, the spectacle of manifestation, the masque and pageantry of the world, conducting the Creator's efforts with divine efficiency.

In the fitness of things; having set up 'Project Creation', Brahma recedes. It is Vishnu who keeps it going, maintains it, preserves it. And when the time comes, consigns it to the abyss of non-being, calling into play, at the precise moment, the forces of destruction that Shiva will unleash before the dark stillness takes over once more.

When all is said and heard, read and considered, the rival schools of theology and philosophy sifted, the conclusion is inescapable—Vishnu has not only an edge over the other two, but leads by several lengths.

The reasons are not far to seek. Both Brahma and Shiva are somewhat unapproachable—one lacks human interest, the other strikes awe and terror into the beholder, with his smouldering third eye which might flash out in a gesture of irrevocable destruction at the switch of a mood. Brahma is somewhat bloodless and the pulsating of sinew, muscle, flesh and nerve that we label as human, fails to respond. There is no answering call of the blood. Shiva, of course, can make one's blood run cold. He catapults us into climes and environs as remote as his ice-covered home, Kailasa. Playing with him is playing with fire and ice.

Vishnu is of this earth and of us. He holds eternity for us in the cupped warmth of his sheltering palm. His weapon, the discus, will spin into action only at the approach of evil, his mace swings out only at inequity. Within him he holds in perfect balance the threat of evil and the wellsprings of good. The coiled serpent of life, *Sesha,* is weighted down and kept in check by his reclining form and his vehicle, the soaring spirit of fire and air, the eagle Garuda, is steered by his expert hand. With his consort Lakshmi ever in attendance, he holds out the promise of peace, plenty, prosperity and well-being. All is under control while the world spins its way on its pre-destined path.

Vishnu's sleep is not the heavy, unheeding slumber of indifference. His slumber is the sleep of restoration and rejuvenation, appropriate for his role as Preserver of the Universe. When the world gets too much for us, when the laws of *dharma,* the rule of life and conduct, are set aside or slacken, when the universe is losing its way and hurtling head-long into confusion and anarchy, Vishnu comes awake and takes note, stepping down from the high pinnacles of divinity into the realms of humanity to set things right or change them.

*Vishnu reclining on the serpent, Sesha; Lakshmi at his feet,
Brahma issuing from his navel*

He is the only god who takes it upon himself to
identify with the human condition, the human
predicament—the only one to take charge, the true refuge
who incarnates to suit a world situation. In the current
mahayuga, comprising four *yugas* of which we are now
in the fourth and last, he has already borne the pain of
nine incarnations or *avataras*—Matsya, Kurma, Varaha,
Narasimha, Vamana, Parashurama, Ramachandra,
Balarama and Krishna. The tenth, Kalki, riding the white
horse of destruction and brandishing a flaming sword,

will preside over the holocaust that sees the end of this cycle. He does not dismiss this world as a trick of *maya* to be borne uncomplainingly. He takes his preserving game seriously.

An anecdote fixes the personality of a god as surely as it does that of a man. An endearing legend recounts the time when Bhrigu was asked in the assembly of gods to decide who was the greatest—Brahma, Vishnu or Shiva. The sage set them a simple test. He first visited Brahma, omitting the usual courtesies. Brahma took umbrage, reacting with anger and abuse. Bhrigu withdrew and proceeded to Shiva, this time behaving even more discourteously. He barely escaped with his life. For Vishnu he preserved his worst behaviour, knowing that he would not be provoked into a show of temper by mere discourtesy. Walking up to his slumbering form, he kicked him rudely awake—only to be anxiously asked if he had hurt his foot! The crown was Vishnu's.

It is significant, this final test of a god—not his strength or power or divinity; just his good temper. The *Vishnu Purana* opens with a paean in praise of good temper: "Anger is the passion of fools; it becomes not a wise man". Which is why Vishnu and all that pertains to him is classified *satvik* (light and pure). Brahma is *rajasik* (dynamic and egocentric) and Shiva, *tamasik* (threatening, menacing).

It is this halo of goodness that establishes Vishnu's supremacy. For the world hinges on a system of moral values and human beings live out their lives on earth sifting good from evil, clearing a path through the tangle of right and wrong. Humanity places a premium on goodness. And the God in charge must keep his temper in times of stress. He must be roused to anger only when he decides to scrap it all, when things are beyond repair.

Of the five human incarnations of Vishnu, two have captured the Indian imagination, perhaps enslaved it, binding it with chains of love and devotion—Rama, Prince of Ayodhya and Krishna, darling of Yashoda, beloved of Radha, King of Dwaraka and later friend, philosopher, guide and war counsellor of the Pandavas. With Ramanuja in the twelfth century, Madhvacharya in the thirteenth and Vallabhacharya in the sixteenth century, *Vaishnavism* spread through the land its honeydew of devotional madness. The poets too caught the inspirational fire—Kalidasa, Vidyapati, Chandidasa, Mirabai and the poet-saints and musicians of the South. The country was swept off its feet in a wave of poetry, song, painting and sculpture that fixed forever in the minds and hearts of devotees the beloved lineaments of Rama and Krishna.

They have inspired our epics, the *Ramayana* and the *Mahabharata,* and given the world an almost irrefutable philosophy of action—the *Bhagvad Gita.* As vehicles of wisdom, good sense, and clear-cut moral guidelines defining the social responsibilities of being human, they form perhaps the complete and ultimate statement. When one has heard what they have to say, there is little more, if not nothing more, to be said on life as it should be lived. There is a splendour and lustre in Vaishnavism that overshadows the severity of Shaivite devotion.

The slumbering form of Vishnu afloat on primordial waters stills the mind, churned by the world into constant turmoil. And as the winds of activity stir him gently awake and the waters move in readiness for a new creation, the promise of better things to come soothes the aching heart of man and fills it with prayer.

Shiva the Destroyer

Arched and curving brow, lips red and softly smiling
moist, cool hair; coral face all smeared with milk-white
ash
left foot glowing, raised in step with time
for the sight of him thus sweetly poised
I crave a human birth again.

— Tirunavukkarasar

Shiva the Destroyer has a divine pedigree that goes
back to pre-Vedic, pre-Aryan times. He must be seen
against the immensity of receding pre-historic dawns,
when the drama of living was played out in primordial
experiences; when mere existence was a wonder, truth
stranger than the fiction of fable.

Shiva is the *Adivasi*, the aboriginal amongst Gods, the
original inhabitant who withstood the Aryan influx and

went underground to emerge and be absorbed in the
Vedic and post-Vedic world views. There clings about
him the hoar of ages, the patina of true antiquity. Shiva,
Mahakala, great conqueror of Time, and therefore of
Death, has made his first conquest—won the battle
for survival.

Creation and preservation, the inevitability of birth
leading to life and ending, or seeming to end, in death,
the story of genesis and the muddle and stumble of life
thereafter, form the stuff of most religions, mythologies,
world-views. Worship and glorification of life-giving,
life-sustaining deities make immediate and comforting
sense. We seek to affirm life as instinctively as a plant
seeks the sun. But the positive role of destruction and
annihilation in the life-process has been rarely as well
and clearly defined as in the Hindu consciousness.
Destruction cleanses, renews, constructs. Destruction
grants the boon of life even as it spells doom and death.
It is the mysterious point at which annihilation meets
being, the pulsating womb-site of the great God,
Mahadeva, Shiva. It is the imperceptible pinpoint where
the external contradictions meet head-on to vanish;
where the simplicity of the human soul stares its own
profundity in the face, acknowledging its reflection, its
image. The appeal of Shiva lies in the utter simplicity of
basic profundities waiting to be grasped, to be realized.

Out of the terrors that swallowed up the seeking
Hindu, out of the volcanic rumblings in the caverns of
his trembling mind, out of his intuitive perception of
destruction as a life-giving, life-breeding force, arose the

Shiva and Parvati; Ganesha (left); Kartikeya (right);
Nandi (right front)

awesome form of Shiva; Shiva who is at once the dance
of death and the dance of life, the end that precedes all
new beginnings.

Shiva's genesis is significant. He enters, howling,
born of the patriarch, Prajapati and the matriarch Aditi.
The source of his discontent was the lack of a name and
his father, quite appropriately, christened him Rudra, the
Weeping One. It was a baptism of tears. Rudra
maintained, through all the stages of his later growth, this
link with his nativity. In the Vedas, this storm of sorrow
took on shades of anger and wrath. The God lived in the

eye of the storm, assuming and assimilating the two most turbulent and rampant elements, fire and water. The concept of Shiva, as it progressed, drew upon Agni, God of Fire, Varuna, God of Water, and Indra, wielder of the thunderbolt. Having gathered unto himself the sound and fury of the storm in which he lived, moved and had his being, Rudra, rider of storms, became its still centre and turned into Shiva, the Auspicious One.

If we consider Vishnu the Preserver and Shiva the Destroyer as contenders for the world's obeisance, we will then see in Vishnu, the extrovert, the charmer, the much-sought-after one. Shiva is the introvert, the loner, an island unto himself, apart, hard to reach and intriguing.

Defiantly non-conformist, counter to all that man is easily drawn to, the worship of Shiva demands an effort that calls into play more than just the simple resonance of a loving soul. Contemplation of Shiva offers no heart's ease. He batters his devotee, blows his mind and boggles his imagination. Scaling the heights of Kailasa, the sights and sounds that greet him are not calculated to soothe. The bellow of his faithful bull, Nandi; his own dread laughter, *attahasa*, freezing into peaks of ice, as described by the poet Kalidasa. The seeker needs to brace himself to bear them as he needs to steel himself to his first vision of Shiva. Matted locks piled high and wild over a forehead bearing a smouldering third eye, softened only by the gleams of the crescent moon, the sway and clatter of his garland of skulls, throat dark with the world's poison, snakes encircling wrists and neck, and his only garment, a tiger skin. From top to toe he is clad in legend that evokes awe, fear and wonder, tales that draw the mind irresistibly with the promise of hair-raising ecstasy. The story of Shiva is high adventure. He lived dangerously and those who brushed with him rarely escaped to tell their tale, or came out winning.

Combats were fierce and bloody. Gajasura, the elephant-demon, was killed, his hide ripped off and held up in a blood-curdling dance of victory. A demon stronghold of three cities threatening to destroy the three worlds was annihilated with a single arrow. A Southern tradition has it that Shiva destroyed all three cities with just a smile in their direction! When the ocean of milk was being churned for the elixir of immortality, a serpent spewed venom into the waters, threatening to taint it. It was Shiva who swallowed the poison and saved the situation. When Ganga came hurtling down to earth to swamp the world with her torrential arrogance, Shiva played saviour. As she vanished into his matted hair she experienced her first moment of humiliation. The God released her on condition that she took a more reasonable and seemly course. When Kartikeya had to be born, Shiva was chosen to father him. Kamadeva, sent to sow the first stirrings of love in Shiva for Parvati, met the fate of all brave and foolish braggarts. Disturbed by unfamiliar, distracting love-thoughts, Shiva looked around, found the culprit, flashed his third eye and reduced the mighty God of Love to a heap of ashes.

Shiva plays a double role, each one a culmination of the Hindu ideal—he is the perfect yogi and the perfect householder. Of the four stages of a Hindu's life-span, student, householder, mendicant and ascetic, the first flowers into the maturity of the second, the third progresses into the ultimate fulfilment of the fourth. The householder and the ascetic or sannyasi are the two high points equally desired and laboured at by the good and god-fearing Hindu. And as the deity that attains both these, and holds them in equipoise, he must necessarily be the complete God.

The destroyer and yogi periodically switches to the softer role of domesticity, conjugal bliss and family life. The courtship of Shiva and Parvati is a tale of true love extending over two life-times. Sati, Shiva's wife in a former age, burnt herself at her father's sacrificial altar when her husband was insulted. She was re-born as Parvati, resisted by Shiva, persisted in her courtship, wooing him with penance and austerities till she won him. Many are the charming tales of the divine couple— their amorous dalliance on snow-clad slopes, their evenings on Kailasa playing dice, their marital spats and sweet reconciliations. Parvati, his beloved Shakti, the power that drove him, took the yogi as she did the householder, working at her marriage like any mortal woman. It is the most successful marriage on record for they were truly one. Shiva, the all-male God, worshipped as the *linga*, the phallic symbol, vindicates the unisex ideal in his aspect of *Ardhanariswara*, half-woman, or man-woman form. It is his tribute to Parvati and their union, and perhaps the perfect answer to today's raging battle of the sexes.

Those who follow Shiva tread strange paths and see strange visions. Shiva is a divine thriller. If the path to Vishnu is strewn with the soft sweetness of lotus petals, the path to Shiva is a roller-coaster ride that jolts the seeker, pitching him into high-altitude conditions that leave him breathless with the euphoria of dread.

Banaras—Dying into Moksha

The thought of Kashi is release
to speak of Kashi is release
to set eyes on Kashi is release
to live in Kashi is release
to bow before a Kashi dweller
that itself bring us release.

—unknown

Each city in India has its own *dharma*, fulfils its own destiny. Mumbai is a boom-metro, bursting at the seams as it goes about the business of commerce. Delhi concerns itself with the karma of governance. Chennai stands still, nurturing tradition with bated breath, uneasy and uncertain. Kolkata still wears the British Raj like a coronet knocked askew, while feebly echoing Raja Rammohun Roy's clarion call for Hindu reform or Vivekananda's missionary blast of Hindu thought.

Banaras goes about its business of life, liberation and death with total self-absorption. Its temples, its schools, its ghats, its cremation grounds, its wrestling academies, its very layout make Banaras, Kashi an inescapable Hindu experience.

To know Banaras is to know the Hindu. Life equals death in the Hindu equation; which is why in Banaras, as elsewhere, the Hindu conducts the business of dying with as much alacrity as the business of living. Living and dying are intervals—one between birth and death and the other between life and life. Both recur in a vicious cycle which all Hindus seek to cut with a final death. For that way lies moksha, liberation. Every Hindu walks in the shadow of this longed-for death that will lead to no more lives. To die in Kashi is to be born no more. It is a city of death with a difference. Here, Yama, god of Death, holds no sway; he is barred entry. Shiva takes over as presiding deity and whispering a mantra into the ear of the dying mortal, ensures oneness with the Brahman.

Banaras has excited wonder, fascination, revulsion and bewilderment in foreign travellers. Keyserling, an Estonian count who wandered the world seeking spiritual experiences, recorded after his visit to Banaras that there, as nowhere else, he "felt nearer ... to the heart of the world." This twentieth-century philosopher who opened a School of Wisdom in Germany after his exile from Estonia, spoke wonderingly of the aura of this city in his "Travel Diary of a Philosopher".

Kashi preserves over 2,500 years of a religious tradition, centred around Shiva. All roads lead to Kashi and all myths gravitate to her. Shiva, inhabitant of the snow-bound peak of Kailasa, chose Kashi as a more fitting abode for his gentle bride, Parvati. He fell in love with the place and like any erring mortal, got what he wanted by somewhat unfair means—by ousting its rightful owner, Divodasa. His dramatic entry into Kashi as a flaming shaft of light which dazzled both Brahma and Vishnu is the enduring myth of Kashi. The glow of this *jyotirlinga*, sign or signal of radiance, lights up Kashi's destiny with a light that never fails. It also evolved into the ultimate phallic symbol. Kashi Viswanatha, as Shiva's sanctum is named here, is one of the twelve *jyotirlingas* spread out all over India. To visit all twelve of them during his or her life-time is every devout Shaivite's dream pilgrimage.

Over the centuries legend gradually populates Kashi with all the gods. And the Ganga, river of heaven, flows sweetly past, washing away the sins of pilgrims forever bathing and praying on the river-front ghats of Kashi. Shiva pervades the whole city and presides over the parallel rise to power of his shakti, energy, power—his Devi, be she Annapurna, Vishalakshi or Kali.

Kashi is the city of light where not only mortals but whole worlds die into salvation at the time of *pralaya*, the great dissolution. Legend also decrees that Kashi, held aloft on Shiva's trident, survives the holocaust to preside over the births, lives and deaths of worlds to come.

Kashi is also a shock that chastens, as one observes the ceremony of death in progress. I once witnessed a cremation at Harischandra ghat. The body was brought, registered, taken down the steps and lay partly immersed with the river softly lapping against it; while the pyre was being prepared the priests haggled with the relatives over the fee. It was a sobering experience, neither revolting nor humiliating, merely eye-opening. It came to me forcibly that life was a deal to be clinched, and so was death; to rage against this fact is futile. One should only try and work out a feasible exit into *moksha*, where all negotiations cease.

Death in Kashi is dealt out as a final and highly desirable deal. No dread end this, only a journey into radiance; perhaps the same that lit up Kashi skies when Shiva first appeared in the city of his choice as a *jyotirlinga*.

THE STORY GROWS

.....and takes shape. Gods and demons proliferate in myth and legend. The hoar of antiquity takes on the flash and sparkle of story. The major epics and story-hoards gather these into themselves as country-wide, poets, seers and raconteurs fashion them into enduring compositions. India speaks the truth of her myth in many tongues and all these tongues ring sweet with the rich sound of meaning.

Lord Subrahmanya asks Avvaiyar:
"What in your eyes is big?" She responds with a

conundrum:
The universe is big, very big indeed
Brahma made the universe
Brahma sprang from Vishnu's navel
Vishnu sleeps on the ocean's surface
the ocean was held in Agastya's belly
that sage was born in a pot of clay
that pot was only a lump of earth
the earth rests on one of Sesha's heads
that serpent's a ring on Uma's little finger
Uma's but half of Shiva's body
Shiva's space is a bhakta's heart
a bhakta's heart is a vast expanse
to speak of that one knows expanse itself.

—Avvaiyar

Ganesha Remover of Obstacles

We'll grasp Ganesha's feet and hold them fast
much good comes of this, so listen, friends
the inner ear will open wide
the inner eye shed radiant light
our minds catch fire with manhood's spark
to help unfurl our victory flags
far and near and everywhere.

— Subrahmaṇya Bharati

A Western philosopher once stated: 'An honest god is the noblest work of man'. He was reflecting the values of his society and times and simultaneously stating a truth, namely, that god is really a human creation. In other words, every culture evolves a god-style.

The Hindu, whose sights are firmly set on the eternally receding, colourless, formless, attributeless, non-beginning, unending state of *moksha* has also devised the most tangible, colourful, variegated, multifarious, delightfully piecemeal, personalised pantheon in the history of religious thought. Besides the main triad, Brahma, Vishnu and Shiva (Creator, Preserver and Destroyer), their consorts, progeny and their various manifestations (not to speak of Vishnu's incarnations) there are wheels within disappearing wheels of deities and divinities that seem to offer all that any human being could possibly fancy in the way of a god.

Along with, or perhaps because of, this bewildering array of forms to worship has arisen the convention of the *ishthadevata*, whereby an individual exercises the privilege of choosing his own god. If tomorrow, the gods and good sense forbid, we were to put the pantheon to vote, Ganesha stands a very good chance of emerging as the winner. That is because he responds to the wide range of everyday, particularly household, needs. He is like a broad-spectrum antibiotic with no harmful side-effects. Kali worship, for instance, gives and takes no quarter. An absent-minded devotee who slips up on even a minor ritual can meet with dire consequences. Not so our vermilion-hued, elephant-headed god, Ganesha.

Ganesha, Ganapati, Gananayaka is lord of the *ganas*, Shiva's motley crew of attendants, and his elder son. Having way back in timelessness conquered Vignasura (demon of obstacles), Ganesha is for all time in charge of that most inescapable of experiences—an obstacle. Life is an obstacle race and the obstacles are negotiable—with Ganesha.

Ganesha

And so, one evokes Ganesha on every occasion—whether it is building a house, learning a new skill or starting a project. The idea being that worshipped and appeased, this rotund, robust and basically benevolent god will remove or at least reduce the obstacles in the path of the supplicant's progress. Ganesha is also in command of power and success, represented in his two consorts, Siddhi and Riddhi. Absurdly, but quite appropriately, he rides his chosen *vahana* (vehicle), the tiny but nimble mouse, for whom no door is ever closed, no crevice or cranny too small to slip through. Between master and attendant (a vahana often doubles up as the deity's assistant and even takes on attributes of his master), no obstacle is too large to surmount, no hurdle too difficult to clear. And the way to success, wisdom, enlightenment, even salvation, lies in the clearing of paths. Hence the all-important position that Ganesha occupies in the pantheon.

The legends about Ganesha range from the sublime to the ridiculous. He pinches sleeping babies and sets them wailing—a gentle reminder to doting mothers who neglect him in favour of their infants. And then there was the time when Shiva offered a delicious fruit as prize to whichever one of his two sons, Ganesha and Kumara, went round the universe and returned first. The earnest, conscientious and somewhat humourless Kumara started off on his journey round the world keeping to, literally and figuratively, the beaten path, while the astute Ganesha cut the proverbial corner, ran round his mother Parvati, claiming that since his mother was the universe he had won the contest.

And, of course, when the learned Vyasa looked for someone to write down the *Mahabharata* as fast as he composed and recited it, Ganesha was the only one who qualified. Ganesha, in turn laid down the formidable condition that Vyasa should dictate without pause and at a speed that would not allow the ink to dry under his pen. So Ganesha is not merely lovable and human or just smart and clever. He is the epitome of all learning and wisdom and the ultimate winner in that competition of competitions—life.

Ancient Indian art and culture have drawn copiously on the gods for subject and inspiration. Our traditional dance, music, poetry and sculpture subsist almost entirely on the seemingly inexhaustible supply of godly antics. It is a tradition that is now beginning to taper. The gods are no longer premium currency for the modern mind—except perhaps for Ganesha. Trunk curled gracefully round a perfect pot-belly resting lightly on plump crossed legs, his image still fascinates the artist, the sculptor, the creative spirit.

Ganesha is free of the mystic, occult obfuscation that tends to cling to our other gods. They seem to need explanation, justification, even an apology to a skeptical generation that leaves nothing unquestioned. Ganesha is an instant sell, with high chances of immediate emotional acceptance. The contemporary, skeptical mind does not snap shut in the face of this one god. And all that the divine duo, Ganesha and his vahana, need is this tiny chink in the modern armour. They are in and firmly entrenched.

Ganapati Pule

Ganapati, Ganesha, Vigneshwara, Vinayaka. Beloved son of Shiva and Parvati. Prime remover of obstacles, auspicious start to all worldly activities. At every turn, one propitiates Ganesha—sculpted, painted, described as the elephant-headed deity, riding his chosen mount, a tiny mouse.

Iconography is a highly developed and complex science in India. Image-makers work to strict rule, meticulously. The making and installing of an idol is as highly skilled and professional an activity as the installation and inauguration of an automobile factory or a computer centre. But, side by side with this, there has been a tradition of *swayambhu murtis*, 'self-created' forms thrown up by nature, untouched by chisel or hammer and identified in mystic visions. They represent man's deep-seated desire to worship something not fashioned by human hands. The rough-hewn weathered *swayambhu murti* leaves everything to the beholder's inner eye. A suggestion of an outline focusses clear as the

conches blow and the temple bells ring for the daily
worship. The joy and wonder of a *swayambhu murti* is
that it exists in the seeking mind and soaring imagination
of the devotee.

All along the coast to Ratnagiri, brown rock and beach
and lonely fortresses speak of brave warriors who fought
and won battles with little to help them except their wits,
their courage and nature's rocky hide-outs. To this
dramatic coastline, washed by the Arabian Sea, belongs
the temple of Ganapati Pule, Ganapati of the Sands, a
hill-side *swayambhu murti*, twenty-five kilometres away
from the mango town of Ratnagiri.

Maharashtra has eight other swayambhu Ganapatis
but Ganapati Pule is a village deity, homely and
accessible, lighting up hearth and home with its friendly
presence.

The legend of Ganapati Pule, its *sthalapurana*, goes
back to a time over three hundred years ago. Those were
troubled times. The splendour of the Moghul court no
longer held the populace in thrall. Its authoritarian
administration was beginning to irk the freedom-loving
people of Maharashtra. Shivaji and his band were
champing at the bit. Town and village alike were rocked
by the tremors of imminent upheaval.

About this time, a young brahmin, Bhide, came to live
in the village adjoining Ganapati Pule. He was the first
brahmin the village had housed. True to his ancestral
disciplines, he countered trouble and turmoil with the
fervour of religious faith and took refuge in meditation
and prayers to Ganesha. His heart was filled with peace

when the deity appeared one night in a vision and bade him look for his divine manifestation on the sea-coast not far away.

Bhide set out for the spot indicated and was faced with a wooded hill. He scanned the hill-side for some sign or likeness of the elephant-headed deity. He did so in vain—till one day, a local cowherd reported a strange incident. One of his cows stopped at a certain spot everyday and let her milk flow, as if to feed the ground she stood on. Bhide decided it was hallowed ground, and clearing the undergrowth, he stumbled upon his vision, half-buried, with the trunk curled in perfect formation, half-way up the hill.

The legend was born, and *swayambhu murti* Ganapati Pule became the presiding deity of the village, blessing them from that hour forth with peace, plenty and inner solace. From a simple rustic shrine it grew to be a prosperous temple—the great Shivaji himself extended his patronage to the family that managed it.

Today, as the devotee walks round the hill completing the ritual circumambulation, praying to the great god Ganesha, the faith of years and the beauty of worship stand over him, shading him from the searing heat of life.

Ganapati Pule has miracle cures and solutions in its repertoire of stories. Incurable disease falls away from a suffering body, leaving it clean and healthy. Childless couples come with despair in their hearts and go back filled with hope and blessed with progeny. The wicked turn over a new leaf and the good are rewarded with prosperity for themselves, kith and kin.

And always, Ganapati, remover of obstacles, clears the path of life on earth, full of stumbling blocks and hidden pitfalls.

Durga, Destroyer of Evil

Shakti is where sorrow dwells not
Shakti is the eye that sleeps not
Shakti is the ripe, sweet fruit of love
Shakti is the rush of manhood, full of power
Shakti is the flare of thought in minds that burn
Shakti is the daily toil, the task at hand
Shakti is release, the end that frees.

—Subrahmanya Bharati

Many dark, primordial moons ago when evil went stampeding through the heavens in the form of Mahishasura, the buffalo demon, the Gods in their hour of need turned to Shiva and Vishnu. The pitch dark of wrongdoing and heedless ignorance was threatening to swallow up the steady glow of right thinking and knowledge. The golden moments of heavenly existence were beginning to show the tarnish of demoniac misconduct. The might of the gods, the *devas*, the shining ones, was in danger of being snuffed out by the misrule of the *asuras*, the anti-gods and demons. The light was going out of their lives.

It was an impassioned plea. Shiva and Vishnu listened with rising concern and mounting disapproval. It was not an unfamiliar situation. Evil always existed alongside good, knowledge beside ignorance in an eternal tantalising tangle. And the universal scales were rarely still in the perfect balance of opposites. But Mahishasura's sway was beginning to strike at the very roots of existence. The cosmic structure was very near collapse.

It was time for drastic action, time to summon up all the strength and power at their command, to call into being a counter-force of light that would end this dark rule of terror.

And so it was that Durga, Mahishamardini, slayer of Mahishasura, came to be. The radiance, the powers, the energies, the *shaktis* of Vishnu, Shiva, Brahma and indeed of the vast assembly of *devas* met in a flash of creation. The darkness that had settled on the world burst open in a dazzle—and of this effulgence was born the sound and fury of blazing wrath that is Durga, difficult to attain, destroyer of difficulties and all evil. Fiery red in hue, clad in the blue of the firmament, her many arms fanned out to fill the sky as she received the martial equipment that each God separately created out of his own special weapon—a trident from Shiva, a discus from Vishnu, a staff of death from Yama, a club from Kubera, a battle-axe from Vishwakarma, a thunderbolt from Indra, and many more. The Gods watched in wonder and relief as she went riding to battle on a rampant lion, her dread laughter mingling with its roar, the three worlds echoing with the sound of fury as she made her way through the Vindhya mountains to seek out Mahishasura.

Durga Puja, Dussera or Navaratri is the celebration of this protracted battle with the forces of evil. Devi, Durga, Bhavani had fought and won other battles. Durga moved Vishnu into waging a prolonged battle with Madhu and Kaitabha, killing Shumbha and Nishumbha who troubled creation with their misdeeds. Many were the dread forms she assumed—Kali, Bhairavi, Chandika as she struck ever-new attitudes of terror and bloody violence. Her battle with Mahishasura was the most critical of all, calling into play every trick, every strategy, every weapon in her armoury. She was all strength and power and swift destruction, tireless in her persistence, unflagging in her zeal, unwavering in the single-minded pursuit of her aim—the destruction of evil. There was no ruse that the demon did not resort to—he was a buffalo, a lion, an elephant in quick succession, baffling her with his rapid changes of form. There was no move she did not make, no skill she did not call forth to counter them. She was prepared, ruse for ruse, and always one up. Her very breath turned into weapons, her looks killed as Mahisha's armies diminished and headless demons died fighting what was clearly a losing battle. The blood and thunder of battle roused Durga into a state of high excitement, and as she quaffed the wine from her goblet,

Durga, Destroyer of Evil

her bloodshot eyes told tales of terror. In a final burst of triumph she pinned Mahiṣha down with her foot, drove the trident into his heaving chest as he strove to hold back his escaping life-breath, her raging lion tearing at his entrails. Thus the demon met his end, gazing into her frenzied eyes; for in their gaze he read both his doom and his deliverance.

Durga Puja is celebrated all over the country but observed with varying rituals regionally, to signify different attitudes. Navaratri, nine nights, is the festival of festivals, devoted overall to this goddess of goddesses who eludes definition as effectively as she outwitted her demoniac opponents. But like all Indian festivals, legends overlap, rituals flower into bunches of variety and many gods step happily into the same act.

In the North, the festival takes a Vishnu slant as the glories of Rama are sung. It is Rama's victory over the demon-king Ravana that forms the fabric of Dussera or Navaratri. But one has only to look a little deeper to realize that the fight is the same, the victory no different, as Rama, the good, retrieves his soul and soulmate, Sita, from Ravana, the demoniac. Rama, in fact sets out with a prayer to Durga and is in truth, right through his life her lieutenant, from his very first *rakshasa* victim to his last and most significant triumph, the killing of the ten-headed anti-god, Ravana, devotee of Shiva and symbol of man's struggle with the demon in himself. The festival ends with the community burning effigies of Ravana, and the deafening sounds of exploding fire-crackers.

In the East, Durga reigns supreme. Simultaneously with the celebration of her as overwhelming power or *shakti*, slayer of Mahishasura and banisher of evil, she is the benign mother and wife who comes visiting her parents' home. She is goddess and woman in one, containing within her all power and all sweetness. Massive images are made by the artisans of Kumartuli who move into Kolkata weeks ahead to shape with loving devotion images of the many-armed Durga. And as the

completed idol is installed in way-side *pandals,*
pavilions, in every neighbourhood, decorated and
dressed with pith-flower garlands and glittering
jewellery, the festive spirit wakens never to slacken
through the entire period of Dussera. Music and fine
clothes and crowds of people moving from image to
image, each one more splendid than the other, turns the
city into a riot of light, colour and gaiety. Celebration
mounts to a fever-pitch of excitement till on the tenth
day, Bijoya, day of victory, she is taken out in procession
and the mood changes to nostalgia as the thought of her
departure—and immersion—approaches. As the river
waters close over her hallowed form, the puja is over, the
victory complete, the visit of a married daughter to her
parents' home concluded—and a fresh year of conflict
and struggle and parting is born anew.

In the South, Durga Puja is a domestic happening. In
Tamil Nadu, rows of dolls and toys in ascending steps
in a room set apart for the celebration make a pretty
picture. As the *kalasha*, the auspicious pot of plenty,
bearing the sacred coconut resting on a ring of mango
leaves is worshipped, the family celebrates. Groups of
girls and boys, dressed in fancy costumes depicting
mythological characters, gods and goddesses, go from
home to home, inviting neighbours and relatives to visit
their *kolu,* their 'doll show'.

The last few days are consecrated to Ayudha Puja
(worship of one's tools of trade)—an all-India ritual, and
Saraswati Puja, when students lay down books much as
warriors lay down arms in the pause between two battles.

It is a renewal of faith and resolution. On Vijayadashami, the tenth and closing day, simultaneous with the victory of Durga, the victory of Saraswati, goddess of learning manifests itself as young and old learn something new, start afresh the quest for knowledge. To a scholar it is a new lesson, to the dancer a new step, to the singer a new song, to the *bhakta* a new chant, to the cook a new recipe, to the scientist a new experiment, to the juggler a new trick. All *vidya*, science of skills, is equal in the eyes of Saraswati.

The nine days and nights of Navaratri are a celebration of the ultimate victory, the only victory worth the fight, the victory of good over evil. Also, as the Hindus conceived it, this battle is prolonged, if not continuous, assuming bloodied and violent aspects terrible to behold, almost unbearable to absorb and at times difficult to comprehend. The black and white of day-to-day existence shade into tones of bewildering grey, the soothing confines of comforting beliefs and common solace break down to open up new, terrifying and receding horizons. Gods begin to overlap, concepts to grow like giants and dwarf the mind, stretching it to breaking point, whirlpools of dilemma dizzy one into a state of churning turbulence, the shifting sands of human pursuits threaten to suck one in and the madness of confusion seems to take over. This is the stuff of which Durga is made—the stuff of eternal challenge and fight and victory; the ugliness and terror that form the morass of the world, out of which, like the lotus out of slush, the beauty of good arises.

The beauty of Durga is the beauty of terror, as befits the consort of Shiva. To comprehend its glory, one has to develop a stomach for strong poison, wipe the mind clean of most accepted norms, hack at the tangled growth of the mind's recesses, learn to pierce the darkness that lies like a pall on our true selves. Only then does Durga stand truly revealed. It is a life-time process, seldom attempted, perhaps never completed but ever relevant.

Agni God of Fire

When Shiva's third eye flashed to strike
Agni's hand could grasp the flame
the sacred fire that sages light
has Agni in their rising flames
thus Agni acts as messenger
from earth to heaven, man to god
in our bellies Agni burns
as hunger and digestive fire
and like a mother, cooks the food
that satisfies and sustains us
Agni lights the ritual fires
that help us see our way through life
and burning up our karmas here
turns them into holy ash.

— Valli Nagappan

Fire plays on the Indian mind, devouring its consciousness and flaming its imagination. From the timeless leap and roar of flame, out of the red flicker of embers glowing to ashen death, from the shadows of the unknown rises the Vedic sacrifice with its ritual fire, invoking Agni, God of Fire, bridging the gap between our world and those beyond. Fanned by seven wind-wheels as he rides his seven-horsed chariot, bannered with smoke and armoured with flame; gold, red, black and tempestuous, with seven tongues, Agni blazes a trail across space, bearing man's hopes and fears and prayers to the powers that be. For the sacrifice is all. Into the sacrificial fire, as the priest feeds it with the fuel of oblation, he pours the very heart and soul of the Hindu. In its ritual roar he strains to catch the sounds of divine response; in its red-gold dazzle are born the visions that make life worth living, death worth dying.

Fire has been wooed by man the world over but few have pursued Agni as constantly, persistently and incessantly as the Hindu. From birth to death and all through life the Hindu reminds himself—and Agni—that they are inseparable. It is a life-long chase—through birth, marriage, festivals, death, through celebration and mourning alike. The domestic fire as well as the ritual fire in all its manifold variations of worship, prayer and incantation is a Hindu obsession; the uses of these to control and direct the fires of the body, the mind, the soul—the fires of hunger, of consuming lust, of rising passion and soaring aspiration, of sublimation, destruction and rejuvenation. For by the light of these fires, some carnal and dread, some golden and healing, others cleansing and purifying, man lives. To be human is to burn—with compassion, with love, with hope, with yearning, equally with envy, greed, wrath, hate and fear. In the ordeal of unending fire that is life, through the mysteries of Agni and by his grace, man can emerge like a bronze image, refined and burnished. Tradition lists forty-nine different fires. Starting with the scorching Sun himself it includes the sound and fury of the thunderbolt and takes in the gentle household fire and the stern funeral pyre that destroys, sanctifies and frees the body from yet another life.

Fire is a witness, and an incorruptible witness at that, from that day in the Hindu consciousness when the following legend took shape. Bhrigu, the great sage, had carried off another's wife. Agni, witness to the incident, told the searching husband where he could find her, thus incurring Bhrigu's wrath. Bhrigu cursed Agni saying that he would be doomed to eat everything, pure as well as impure. When Agni pointed out the unfairness of this outburst, Bhrigu softened the curse by pronouncing that impurities would turn pure on entering Agni. All believing Hindus call upon Agni to stand witness, or *sakshi*, to important events in their lives.

Fire is also light. A voracious and indiscriminate eater, Agni is at his glowing best when he swallows darkness, eats into gloom, and chases away the shadows of fear, doubt and evil that threaten to overcome humanity.

Divali is the festival of fire and light. The skies brighten and echo to endless fireworks as Hindus re-establish links with their Vedic beginnings, and renew hope in a world full of the despair of eroding and suppurating values. Our world is eating into us—its darkness, its dread, its corrosive evil. More than ever, light needs to be thrown over the obscure and menacing pitfalls that humanity has dug for itself in the pursuit of material progress. Hope lies in the light that can fill the heart of man, the light of ideas that can crackle and burst into flame, the Agni of salvation. And Divali, when fire is a palpable presence, is a time for minds to catch fire and souls to keep warm in the glow of customary celebration.

Ours is a heritage of light. We have enough wisdom to see by. The attics of Indian thought are still capable of yielding up treasures to those who are willing to rummage. Our gods may be languishing, but the ideas from which they sprang have centuries of wear in them still. The celebration of light at least will not suffer from obsolescence, for every Divali is a beating back of the powers of darkness by a general heartening consensus of opinion.

Lakshmi Goddess of Prosperity

In gold, in gems, in scents of flowers
in sandal paste and shining lamp
in smiles of girls, in forests lush with growth
in groves of soothing shade, in fertile fields
in faces stamped with courage
in the countenance of kings
in these she dwells, this holy one.

— Gnanasambandar

Lakshmi, synonymous with *Shri*, lustre, is the wife of Vishnu, the Preserver—and that indefinable but unmistakable spirit that every household tries to capture and keep captive with a hundred ritual ruses. She is what blesses a hearth and turns a house into a home, the blessed touch that transmutes four walls and a roof into the living warmth of a beckoning threshold. She is the promise of peace and plenty and sweet fulfilment, the mellow tint of dreams come true, the golden glow of happiness. Lakshmi is the goddess of good fortune, not merely of fortune; she is wealth not merely riches. She is all that prospers.

Lakshmi is the most powerful weapon in her husband's armoury as he goes about the unending task of preserving and maintaining the world, the life-force that infuses humanity with the will to go on, the zest for living that counters world-weariness. As Vishnu slumbers through interludes of recuperation, she is awake and on guard, pressing the Lord's feet weary with treading the world's thorny paths, reviving with her touch the myriad impulses that need to quicken in the Preserver's being as he goes about his business of world-management. She has in her keeping the life-breath of Vishnu, its mysterious rhythms. While he sleeps, she is his consciousness, when he wakes and steps out, she is by his side, ever in step with his plans for the welfare of humanity.

Lakshmi is in full command of the many schemes devised by Vishnu for the physical, mental, emotional and spiritual well-being of humanity. She assumes responsibility for their effective execution, making sure that they touch all aspects of man's life on earth, all that adds to good and right living, making life on earth a rewarding experience in the expanse of eternity.

Lakshmi is the unmistakable stamp of success on all worldly ventures—and this extends beyond, much beyond, material success. It covers matters of the mind, the intellect, the heart, the senses. Lakshmi is as simple or as complex as we want her to be. She is as much or as little, as big or as small, as extensive or as limited, as manifold, as unvarying, as shifting, as fixed, as far-reaching, as confined as each individual wishes her to be. To each his or her own Lakshmi. To some she is Vijaylakshmi, the triumph of success; to others Rajalakshmi, the glory of success; to yet others Varalakshmi, the granter of boons; and to most, Grihalakshmi, the success of a happy home.

Grihalakshmi is the most endearing and sought after of Lakshmis. A good household concentrates all its energies on luring her into its confines and charming her into staying. Besides the prescribed pujas there are many ways to attract Lakshmi, to catch her attention—happy children, smiling faces, shining doorsteps, the sights, sounds and smells of good housekeeping. Lakshmi is felt, perceived and desired not only by good Hindus or even Indians—she is a world-fact, a universal concept. It was an English poet, the greatest of them, who provided me with my first perception of Grihalakshmi—in the concluding song of Puck, the fairy, in Shakespeare's *A Midsummer Night's Dream*, a song which surely must be a hymn to Grihalakshmi: "And we fairies, that do run.../ Following darkness like a dream/. Now are frolic. Not a mouse/ Shall disturb this hallowed house./ I am sent with broom before/ To sweep the dust behind the door".

Lakshmi embraces all aspects of life on earth, adding the success dimension to any venture, even adventure. As a Hindu progresses through the four prescribed stages of life on earth—student, householder, recluse, hermit,

Lakshmi progresses to fulfil his changing needs. And there is no stage at which she does not stand by, for success and good fortune must attend all human activity. Growth, involvement, maturity, even withdrawal and cutting loose require her blessing, her aid. She is money when you need it, learning when you desire it, salvation when you seek it; contentment, joy, fulfilment of any aim, all aims that are laid down for the conduct of living.

If Lakshmi is the truth of success, she is also the truth of beauty. In her, too, truth and beauty meet in lustrous union. She bursts upon the world in all her golden glory, thrown up by the mythical churning ocean of milk, borne aloft on creation's lotus. Beauty is in the mind's eye and in the eyes of the beholder. And when the mind and eyes are Vishnu's, perfection prevails.

One must end with a charming poetic fancy by the mystic, Rahim, which reminds one of the very earthly, earthy nature of Lakshmi. As the goddess of fortune, she eludes our grasp. Her restlessness is well-known. She comes very rarely to stay—and needs to be eternally chased. And this, says Rahim, is because she has for husband an ancient man!

Divali, Festival of Light

Shridevi, holy, golden one
yourself a lamp that brightens dusk
gem-set, bedecked and beautiful
shall have my lamp of purest gold
placed in sacred, patterned space
with cotton wick all steeped in ghee
and in the light of its pure flame
will glow our lineage, hearth and home
for you will shower wealth on us
children, livestock, ornaments
and even as you bless this house
you shall make my heart your home.

— unknown

The West has spawned a spate of fun things—learning must be fun, teaching must have a plethora of aids, pills must be sugar-coated, multi-coloured and a soft-pedalling of reality. The East, in particular India, has in its wisdom and good sense put its finger on the cure for worldly ailments, the answer to life on earth—a workable, hardcore religious base that comes clothed in pageantry—the pageantry of gods, temples, festivals and household ritual, an enchanting stairway to salvation. No other culture has devised a pantheon that caters to such a wide range of taste in matters divine, or allows so boldly for human caprice in matters of worship. It would have to be a truly cussed Hindu who can reject the entire pantheon and turn atheist; for in the face of a religious philosophy that holds out the promise of an attributeless Absolute as the ultimate goal and a multitude of paths to get there, we must believe—or else feel faintly foolish.

Divali, festival of lights, comes in with the first nip in the air. Divali is a flash of light, a burst of sound, a river of joy that washes away the cares and pains of day-to-day existence. Divali is the victory of light over dark, knowledge over ignorance, life over death, vision over mystery. As the year progresses to Divali, there is a dawning of reassurance. For good is stealing a march over evil, wisdom over folly, success over failure. Divali is a magical evocation of the forces of well-being through the time-honoured, hallowed methods of persuasion and cajolery. It is a ritual largely calculated to propitiate the Goddess of Fortune, Lakshmi.

You can take your pick of Divali legends—just as different parts of India did. In the North it commemorates the victory of the god-King Rama of Ayodha, Vishnu incarnate, over the demon-King Ravana of Lanka—in an epic war waged over the abduction of Sita, Rama's wife, Lakshmi incarnate. In the South, Divali celebrates the death of the demon Narakasura at the hands of Krishna, Vishnu incarnate. In the East, Divali is propitiation of Kali, the fearsome aspect of Devi, a primal female force that strikes terror into the hearts of all evil-doers. Kali is power in action, roused to the point of destructive no return at the sight of evil. As a preventive measure, the annual summoning of Kali to the minds of erring humanity has few equals. In the West it is largely a paean of praise to the glory of Lakshmi in her aspect as Goddess of Wealth. Money and trade are glorified and the bazaars come alive to see out an old year of good business and usher in a new year of better trading. Appended to the New Year is *Bhaiduj* a day when sisters greet brothers with ritual affection and renew their life-long lease of brotherly protection. Yami, it is believed, visits her dread brother Yama, God of Death, on this day.

It is good to remind oneself that whenever a god wages war on a demon, or a demon is outwitted by a god, it is a score for goodness; for instance when, according to yet another Divali legend, Vishnu in the form of a dwarf tricked the demon-King Mahabali into exile. If the world is to progress, the scoreboard must always register one up for goodness. Evil is kept at bay by methods and measures devised by human beings in collusion with the gods.

Divali is, therefore, an annual expression of faith in not so much the good things of life but the right things of life. And within general and widely applied socio-religious norms there are regional variations, arising out of value systems and priorities that reflect a regional turn of mind.

Like all our festivals, Divali has two layers—one religious, the other secular. The gods are attended to with the appropriate pujas, lighting of lamps, showering of flower petals, ringing of bells, the holy smoke of burning incense and the flare of camphor set alight for the puja. All this is led up to with the ritual bathing and cleansing of oneself and the implements and images of household worship. With the heart and mind emptied of niggling pre-occupations, the family does obeisance.

Discipline has been exercised over the restlessness that is the most widely prevalent human disease. You gather your drifting wits and focus them on a point of divinity—be it Lakshmi, Krishna, Rama or Kali, in a manner laid down by your region, your people. Having done your duty to your God, you turn outward, face the world squarely and shoulder the responsibilities of right and good living. You celebrate life, and there is no better way to celebrate life than to feed the five senses. Divali satisfies them in a way that few other festivals do. It is an audio-visual feast, a *son-et-lumiere* fit for the gods—lights that dazzle you into a state of mild euphoria, new clothes that flatter the body, fireworks that startle you into a state of high ecstasy, sweetmeats that satiate the palate.

Divali begins long before the actual day with a pleasant sense of anticipation, the planning and choice of clothes, the buying of burnished metal utensils, the making of store-away foods; and the cracker-bazaars that spring up turning whole rows of shop fronts into a Divali spectacle.

The buying tempo mounts; clamouring children reach out for every new firework idea that shops offer; indulgent parents throw thrift and caution to the winds as they buy dreams of their own charmed childhood, dreams etched in sparklers and filled with the sounds of past Divalis—the crack and flash of red paper circlets, the garlands of pin-crackers that are drowned in squeals of childish delight, the rockets that zoom into limbo with a clap of muffled thunder. And everywhere the humble mud lamps, diyas, bought up in dozens, that will transform the dark night of a new moon into a poem of light.

Such is Divali—the spirit of joy in goodness, a concerted effort to combat darkness and sorrow, a haven of radiance carved out of the terror that life can be. And the spirit survives—survives high-rise living that often turns this dream of light into a nightmare of fear; when, for lack of space, fireworks go off on pigeon-hole verandahs and fire engines wait in readiness to cope with the many accidents that have become an invariable part of celebration.

Perhaps a big-city Divali where millions are gambled away, sent up in smoke or shamelessly flaunted, is something that this festival with its many presiding deities can contain. If humanity can play host to a god as gentle as Rama, applaud a killing Krishna and make bold to receive the red-tongued, bloodied, frenzied image of Kali, it can forgive and tolerate the less pleasing manifestations of the human predicament.

Lakshmi is beguiling, and at times heedless. Those who receive her favours do not always wear them lightly or gracefully. Lakshmi comes in many ways, many forms. She is the soft radiance of contentment, the brazen shine of new wealth. She is the golden blessing of household happiness or the gentle glow of a fulfilled life. She is the flash and sparkle of success. She is all these—and so is Divali, her special feast.

The Ramayana–Epic of All Time

Those who saw his shoulder saw nothing else those
who looked upon his lotus feet, their gaze was held
those who glimpsed his mighty arm, were likewise
trapped
whose long and lovely eye was it
that ever saw his whole vast form?

— Kamba Ramayanam

The *Ramayana* is undoubtedly among the world's most widespread and unforgettable epic poems. There are seventeen major *Ramayanas* adapted from Valmiki's original in the various Indian languages and dialects; and Buddhist and Jain versions too. *The Ramayana* also travelled abroad with the southern Indian maritime empires and took root in South East Asia in modified forms to fit in with alien cultural modes. *The Ramayana* thus seems to have been a cultural and spiritual resource for more than one country and more than one faith. It was composed nearly three thousand years ago and has survived an oral tradition that could have chosen to forget it. It is celebrated not because of its storyline, a common enough tale of heroic feats, kings, queens and demons; of battles with fabled monsters and war with an island kingdom and its demon king, Ravana, over the abduction of a princess, Sita, wife of Rama. It is remembered because of the moral and spiritual message that strains though its 24,000 verses of exquisite poetry whose very stanzaic metre was born in a burst of compassion in its author, the sage Valmiki. He had heard the birdcry of agony let out by the female of a pair of mating herons when the hunter's unfeeling arrow pierced the male in the very act of union. That set the emotional tone for the whole work.

I have said elsewhere that Rama 'is a lesson in that most obsessive of ancient Indian pre-occupations— dharma ... The Ramayana is ... a treatise of high thinking. It is the Indian book of values in which dharma, the code, is all.' It is, along with the Vedas, the Upanishads and the Mahabharata, India's offering to world thought.

To perceive the continuing relevance of the Ramayana one has to acknowledge the Indian time-set. Time moves not in a straight line but in circles, in recurrent circles at that. One does not look straight ahead till the future vanishes out of sight or straight back till the past recedes. One looks round a curve and waits for time to come full circle as it inevitably does. The Indian psyche does not shed the past but waits for it to catch up with the present and turn gently into the future. For this mind-set, trashing the past is wasteful, recycling it is productive. In this context one should pay heed to the Indian definition of an ancient text, i.e. a *Purana*. 'Pura api nava' is the etymological splitting of the word-compound in Sanskrit. Literally, 'new although old'. Most of what the Indian has enshrined had to pass this test. Relevance was therefore inbuilt as in some industrial activities obsolescence is inbuilt. In our cyclical continuum the crucial question is not "Is it new, is it novel?" The question to ask is "Is it enduring, does it fit?"

Time, and therefore life or creation, proceeds in cycles. Creation is also, according to the Hindu perception, *leela*, the sport and pastime of a creator bored, restless and in terror of loneliness. From the unmanifest, therefore, the manifest. From the manifest, the manifold, the varied and the variegated, the colours of life.

An era or *yuga* is a die cast in this game of creation. Each age actually gets its name from gambling terminology. The ideal, the luckiest, the perfect throw is the *kruta*. In the *Krutayuga* or *Satayuga*, as it is sometimes termed, right is might beyond question. The next throw, less than perfect, a quarter less, in fact, the *treta*, gives us the *Tretayuga*. The cracks begin to appear, blessings come mixed and disguised. Principles gather a slight mist, haze over, visions are clouded. Rama of the Raghu dynasty ruled in such an age. But things were still under control. Might was not quite right and if it tried to be, as Ravana learnt at the cost of his ten mighty heads, right or Rama rose to quell it—successfully. With the third throw, *dwapara,* we have time and life spinning dangerously, calling for urgent action. For we are now only half of what we should be. We are in the *Dwaparayuga,* the age of Krishna, when the game of life is threatened with defeat and disasters to come. Might is making disquieting headway and right is no longer so confident of victory. Krishna incarnates, as the *Bhagvad Gita* states explicitly in one of the clearest manifestos ever, to re-establish *dharma,* right, for the very foundations of existence were being rocked. The fourth and final throw, *kali* (our current situation) is the foretold bad end. There is little to save, only a modicum. Right is not floundering but drowning, in the *Kaliyuga.* The voice of unrighteousness is heard loud and clear and *dharma* is a lone, fading echo in the wilderness. Dissolution, *pralaya,* is in sight and, of course, following that a fresh round of hope, of time, of life, with the same erosive process to follow.

It is possible to fit history into this perception of zenith and nadir, crest and trough, rise and fall. To examine ancient models of conduct, of government, of social order, is educative. The workings of a well-ordered polity, be it through dynastic succession or elected governments, have always stood on a base of principles, a bedrock of ministers and advisors, a fabric of politicians and administrators who guide or misguide the fortunes of the populace. It was so in the *Tretayuga* under the dispensation of the Raghus. It is so now.

Raghurajya, or *Ramarajya* as it has come to be known after Rama, speaks with surprising relevance of patterns and models applicable even now. Human nature calls for the same skills in handling similar situations. Societal conditions only call for fresh approaches. The chronic, the critical is upon us but the human condition is the same, the methods used to hold the malaise in check still apply. The difference is only in who wields power and with what intent, the quality of leadership, the calibre of the guiding lights. W.B. Yeats has said of our times in his poem, 'The Second Coming'—'The best lack all conviction while the worst are full of passionate intensity'. Our Kali comes riding a white horse, brandishing a sword; Yeats's dark, menacing *tamasic* figure, 'slouches towards Bethlehem to be born.'

Dasharatha's, and after him Rama's, aims were underlined and emphasised, even overstated. Dasharatha was known throughout the world, says Valmiki, for battling in the cause of *dharma* or right. His mental, emotional and spiritual resources were as vast as his material and temporal strengths. Those were the requirements of the age. He had to measure up to a demanding populace. Their expectations ran high and their approval supported and reinforced him. Then as now, power fed on popular mandate. In the world's biggest democracy, that should be a sobering thought.

Here, one of the incidental debates of our times should be examined—age versus youth. There is much talk of fresh blood, young ideas, youth power. The youth image dominates. Youth is equated with energy, drive and progress. *The Ramayana* on the other hand seems to thrive on old age. Rama's father Dasharatha, at the time of abdication had ruled for 60,000 years, not to be taken too literally, of course, with a council of ministers who were not too young or sprightly either. They were a bunch of elder statesmen who were philosophers, intellectuals and sages. But here lies the crux of the selection process; they had spent those long years on the gathering of knowledge, of skills, of insights, of experience. Age added an invaluable dimension, wisdom, that intangible function of the inner eye. One cannot learn wholly on the job. One has to observe from the wings, ingest, before one comes on stage.

This is not to say that the times disqualified youth. Rama was an exception that proved the rule. He was a precocious youngster who managed to pack in the experience, knowledge and wisdom of many life-times into a short span of existence. Everybody sees it and remarks upon it. His brothers, his sisters, his teachers, the court. Here again it is worthwhile remembering that not only had he to be exceptional and recognised as such by his father and advisors, he had to be seen and known to be so by the people of Ayodhya. They greeted his succession with vociferous and uncontained joy. They clamoured for his coronation. Rama had already given them a show of his strengths. But those strengths amounted to little without a surge of popular acceptance. Their grief when he was exiled by a palace intrigue went beyond the limits of ordinary disappointment. Modern ministerial resignations in India that are followed by instant comebacks at the slightest persuasion stand out in sharp contrast to Rama's steadfast refusal to be reinstated. Circumstances had edged him out and his exit was prompt and glorious—he resisted his father's plea to stay for just a day longer.

Even more interesting is the detailed and graphic listing of a good minister's qualities. Dasharatha's success is attributed to his council of advisor-ministers. What heads the list is significant; the humility of great learning, and modesty. Then follow skills of governance and politics, valour and heroic traits, a good reputation, gifts of diplomacy, an aura, a lustre, an inner energy and drive, readiness to attack, readiness to protect; single-minded devotion to duty, constant concern with justice and fairplay even towards the enemy, patience, forbearance and political stamina. They were wily enough to tackle political exigencies, respected, admired and feared beyond the frontiers of their own kingdom, knowing when to initiate peace as well as war.

The image was not all character, expertise and spiritual insight. There was a public relations angle too. They were well-dressed, well-groomed, persuasive and sweet of speech, subtle. They kept themselves well informed of happenings both domestic and external, through a network of spies. But they operated within the strictest of moral codes where integrity (which is not always defined by the narrow limits of honesty) decided all matters. In other words, your ends had to be transparent, your means equally so. The permissible was clearly indicated and accountability had a way of catching up with truants. Theory went roughly along with practice and practice with preaching.

The advisory role seemed to feature large in their scheme of things. And rule was by consensus too. Among the searching questions that Rama puts to his brother Bharata who ruled in his absence is "Do you rule with collective good counsel or do you rely too much on a single opinion, your own at that?" This is effectively demonstrated later when Ravana, well-versed in all branches of knowledge, proclaims in a pompous opening speech at a war council, that consultation is the key to victory. He even defines the sources of such consultation: professionals, friends and well-wishers, kith and kin. He knew it all, at least the theory. He who sets out after weighing all three types of advice, says Ravana, is truly *purushottama,* best among men. One who relies only on himself rates second and one who fails to follow up is truly inferior. Advice also falls into three categories. The highest is that which is based on traditional wise tenets and results in a unanimous decision. The next best is one that reconciles varying opinions into an acceptable compromise. The worst is debate and consultation that is inconclusive and therefore, by implication leads to inaction, the worst possible alternative in a crisis. Today's parliamentary proceedings, inquiry commissions and committees seem to accomplish just this.

There is a lesson to be learnt here. Ravana gives a hearing to patently good advice and spurns it. At least three separate assessors, his wife and his two brothers, advised him to return Sita and make peace. Fight only to lose, they all declared. He bullied and intimidated his court and his counsellors into consensus, but a consensus that furthered only his personal ends and delusions of grandeur. The counsellors tried, but failed in their job and so did Ravana, led by his demoniac ego. All was certainly not well in the state of Lanka. He ultimately hears only what he wants to hear and pays the price. Might, since it was the Tretayuga, was working towards its own downfall by playing into the hands of Right.

Getting back to the profile of an ideal minister, Hanuman is intended as a supreme example. It is significant that he arrests Rama's attention almost immediately with his manner and conduct, though he was disguised as a mendicant. We all get an insight into the importance of a messenger-ambassador. Hanuman goes straight to the point, shoots off questions and introduces himself with a cultured assurance and elegance that makes a strong impact. Rama assesses him as learned, impressive with a distinctive, concise and effective delivery, an attractive and pleasing personality, a clearly modulated voice that charms and entices the listener. He ends by saying that a king with such an emissary is assured of success in all his undertakings. In fact, using Hanuman as an indicator, Rama decided that Sugriva, king of the monkey-tribes, would indeed be instrumental in defeating Ravana and freeing Sita.

There is no doubt that the profile of Hanuman, Sugriva's minister, was a role model. Valmiki dwells on this theme. Hanuman's thorough survey of the situation in Lanka, his sensitivity to Sita's plight, his strategy when he found her, all bear testimony to a sophisticated, intuitive and able representative. After spotting Sita and the gentle handling of a fragile situation, he does not sit back and say 'mission accomplished'. He ponders and speculates on what more could be done. He decides that a foretaste of things to come, a show of strength was called for and destroys Ravana's prized wooded park, leaving unscathed, tellingly, only the spot where Sita stood. As intended, the news reaches Ravana. Hanuman gets an even better idea. Allowing himself to be captured, he finds himself in the presence of Ravana, unthinkable in normal circumstances. It was an opportunity to assess the situation from within. And then, counting on Ravana's ego, he invites humiliation, even death. With his tail set on fire by Ravana's orders Hanuman, son of the wind god, wreaks havoc as he goes through the city, fanning the flames. Leaving the enemy in confusion and some panic, he returns to Rama. All through, Valmiki provides the lineaments of a minister and ambassador that could serve well even today.

As do his women. Sita, wife of Rama was no meek, submissive partner. True, she declared that she would walk in Rama's footsteps. But she did so out of choice and at times against his specific wish, even command. She followed him into the forest not by subjugating her individuality or by erasing it, but by asserting it. She spurned the comforts of the palace since her husband was foregoing them and demanded equal rights to both his joys and his travails.

Sita never hesitated to speak her mind. Rama, while in exile, had undertaken to guard some special weaponry handed over to him by Indra. Sita tells him he is wrong to take on such tasks while on a spiritual journey. By sheer association, his thoughts, she said, would turn to violence. His war-like instincts would be roused at a time when he should be focussed on the inner life.

Mandodari, Ravana's wife, was equally a person in her own right. She predicted that in wooing Sita he was courting disaster and advised him against his folly. As she mourned Ravana, she spoke of his love for her, his desire, his drunken, roving glances. She was no wife who merely awaited her lord's pleasure but was an active partner in their life together. Neither Sita, wife of the righteous Prince Rama, nor Mandodari, wife of the redoubtable, ten-headed demon-king Ravana, were shy, retiring damsels in a state of seemly distress. They were full-blooded, vibrant, dynamic women. The surrendering, unquestioning Sita of Kamban and Tulsi, later Ramayanas of the tenth and fifteenth centuries A.D., towering in their literary and spiritual stature, were not examples of submissive Indian womanhood. They entered on the tidal wave of *bhakti,* ardent devotion to a chosen deity; *bhakti* that turned Valmiki's ideal super-king and hero into a god. *Bhakti* demanded unquestioning faith and unconditional surrender from women as well as men—Hanuman, Lakshmana, Vibhishana (Ravana's brother). To twist devotee figures into submissive female role models was a trick of social history and male chauvinism. Neither Kamban nor Tulsi intended anything of the kind.

Ramarajya, which was the point of the *Ramayana*, was built up over generations of *Ikshvakus*, the famed clan of Raghu and Rama. The torch of *dharma*, right, was handed down and kept alight, flaring into exceptional brilliance with some rulers. Tradition is repeatedly invoked along with the good name of the Raghus, their prowess, their past feats. The lessons of the *Ramayana* belong to no religion, deified though Rama may be. They are part of the Indian consciousness and an occasional plunge into our past perceptions might direct our energies to positive goals, clear our apathies and confusions and restore equilibrium.

I end with a quote from the introduction to my rendering of the Valmiki *Ramayana*—'We move in the lengthening shadows of a moral twilight and before us looms the darkness of dead and dying values. We clutch at the straw of amorality that excuses and condones the evil in ourselves and others. We live uneasy lives, shutting out the blinding glare of truth, the searchlight of morality. Our world is an area of grey, slipping into darkness. The story of Rama ... is one of India's hidden weapons, performing unseen wonders, providing unknown strengths.' To read about times when sights were clear and priorities even clearer, is elevating. And what elevates is bound to improve.

The Ramayana is indeed relevant—to all people, anywhere, but particularly in the land of its birth, and particularly now. India is under serious attack from within and the issues are beyond question, moral. The remedy too must lie within. It is the spirit of India that needs to be healed.

Indian Womanhood–The Myth

Women should not read, said some
their breed has vanished, this we know
men lead, control and strike their herds
drive them in and tether them
thus they treat their women too
cut their shackles, dance with joy
even as you set them free
and matrimony forced, unjust
we'll knock it down and stamp it out.

— Subrahmanya Bharati

She has been over three thousand years in the making. She is a myth with an elaborate and complex ground-pattern woven into, at various stages, by the *Vedas*, the *Puranas*, the epics and continuing legend. Following her like reflections in a charmed and mirrored hall are her earlier likenesses. The contemporary Indian woman walks in the shadow and lustre alike of this heritage. For myth in India is living and doggedly persistent. What the Indian woman shrugs into place on her strong, broad shoulders is a mantle of inherited paradox that drapes well and gracefully.

Let us start with Sita, the very soul of unquestioning acceptance—till, that is, her integrity is over-questioned. She spent the prime of her householding life quite willingly wandering in the forest with a husband who, instead of fighting for his rights, gave up his throne in the face of blatant emotional blackmail. Her only show of strength, which must have taken Rama completely by surprise, was her single and final act of rebellion when she refused to prove her chastity with a second ordeal by fire. It was a dramatic rejection of her lord and master. She disappeared, leaving no room for further negotiation, into the receiving arms of her mother, Prithivi, Earth who opened up to swallow her. She was back home. It was perhaps the first Indian matrimonial walk-out.

Draupadi, wife of the Pandava princes, took on five husbands, three of whom were larger than life— Yudhisthira, model of righteousness, Bhima, strongman who flexed his muscles and went into gallant and chivalrous action at her least command and Arjuna, superman and warrior, star-pupil of Dronacharya and the one chosen by Lord Krishna himself to receive the formidable philosophic onslaught of the *Bhagvad Gita*. She managed them all and made a difficult and unconventional marriage work like a dream, even though there were times when it was very rough going; as for instance, when Yudhishthira lost her to the Kauravas in a game of dice. In open court, as the Kauravas prepared to claim her with insulting and humiliating gestures, she raged against her situation, pointing an accusing finger at her husbands as they stood mutely by, honouring Yudhishthira's pledge. She taunted them with the ultimate insult—impotence. And she got away with it. She made it with Sita and three others with equally non-standard qualifications to the traditional panel of the five ideal women, the *Panchakanyas*.

Savitri married Satyavan in the full knowledge of certain widowhood, a most dreaded Indian condition. She crossed that bridge when she came to it. It was no ordinary bridge; it was the bridge of death. She argued, harangued and finally outwitted Yama himself. "Bless me", she said, making out that she was giving up; and the mighty God of Death relaxed his guard briefly, perhaps in sheer relief at the end almost in sight. "Of course, go right ahead and ask". "Bless me", she said, "with many sons". Surely, Yama could not bless her with progeny born of widowhood. So Satyavan lived, and Savitri proved that nothing, literally nothing is impossible. Strength of mind, particularly, could work miracles.

As Parvati, daughter of Himavan, King-Emperor of mountains, proved. She had fallen in love, quite unaccountably, with the strangest of yogi-mendicants. He wore garlands of skulls and live snakes and sat with his three eyes closed in reputedly unbreakable meditation. Altogether a fearsome and undesirable bridegroom for this cherished flower of the mountains. But she had set her wayward heart on him. And she did not give up. Not even when at the first unwelcome stirrings of a faint response, he flashed his third, dread eye, reduced Madana, the God of Love, to a heap of ashes and strode off, spurning her. The challenge was met. She gave up girlhood pleasures and pastimes, wooed him with severe penance till he was won. Whoever said Indian women are coy and bashful?

And there is, of course, the most enduring of Indian concepts—the concept of woman as *shakti* or power, evoked and released at moments of crisis by the very gods themselves. Like Durga, brain-child of the pooled effulgence of all the gods, summoned to exterminate Mahishasura. As she waxes in power in her battle for the triumph of good over evil, she assumes ever more terrible forms—Kali and Chamundi.

Shakti can also be benevolently forceful, working in unison with the male, in what was aptly referred to at the Transpersonal Conference in 1982 by June Singer as 'the yoga of androgyny', Shiva-Ardhanarishwara, Shiva-Parvati. It is a male recognition of female indispensability that rises above, even disowns, gallantry, chivalry and other romantic pitfalls. It is most certainly not a male ruse for hoodwinking women into not fighting for their rights. I suspect that Women's Lib and feminism, in their western expressions, will falter in embarrassment when they encounter this wise and difficult-to-fault expression of woman-power. Militant feminists in India even as they scream out their demands might find, both in principle and in practice, that much has already been conceded by Indian tradition. It pays to be traditional. We should source our own prototypes.

And one must not forget Saraswati, *Vak*, speech, and that first and most treasured application of the primordial sound of creation, Om. Saraswati is the prime instrument of knowledge and percipience, understanding and wisdom, and the Creator's first temptation. As a concept, it is even more of a compliment to womanhood than even Shakti.

The image of Indian womanhood survives because it stretches to include timeless and, therefore, modern and contemporary needs and exigencies. It was gradually and continually fashioned to accommodate a universal form and has a built-in resistance to obsolescence. There is a lot to leave but enough to take and carry on. It escapes the iconoclast because it does not invite destruction. It is a concept expressed in varied, persuasive, convincing statements and essentially free of dogma. It has room and space for future models. Like most things in India, or the womb itself, it is conducive to birth and growth and resistant to death. Which is why it is continuing. The last word on Indian womanhood will never be pronounced, for such a thing, to the pragmatic Indian consciousness, spells death. There is only a living, growing idea seeking fresh articulation.

Indian Motherhood—The Myth

The hand that once held out food to our mouths
has only to point and we'll swallow live coals.

— Subrahmanya Bharati

At birth she brings a burden of sorrow
in youth anxiety for her good name
at the time of marriage, deprivation of wealth
she tears at the heart, indeed, her father's heart!

— Sanskrit verse on a daughter

'... This breast of yours, unfailing, refreshing, bearing treasures, giving of largesse by which all that is choicest in the world is nourished, may you nourish, O Saraswati ... you have given birth to a hero and thereby attain heroic stature...'

Thus ends an ancient household rite, described in great detail, for a male child. It is in fact the only point in the whole proceedings, starting with the actual act of intercourse and ending with the placing of the son on her lap, at which the woman receives a measure of affectionate attention. She is simultaneously deified too, in the true Hindu manner. She has, to use a managerial euphemism, been kicked upstairs.

It is as if the moment she lactates, the male milk of human kindness also begins to flow, presumably to dry up once again till the next lactation and the next son. And we must remember, these were times when coinage was, literally, a cow. Yajnavalkya, the great wandering scholar was paid in cows. "I give you a thousand cows", King Janaka declared. This was the fee for instruction in *brahma vidya,* the science of truth.

I say 'woman' only in a manner of speaking. The invocation is a classic instance of the whole standing for the part. For the glorification here is of the breast. For 'breast' read 'udder' and we have the beginnings of the bovine ideal for women, the role model that the Indian woman has been brainwashed into following—the nourishing, contented, mooing companion-through-life, stroked lovingly when she conceives to good purpose, that is, when she produces a son; and indulgently tolerated when she produces a daughter. We know, too, that things can turn quite ugly if she persists in giving birth to female infants.

Indian cinema, which very often is a reflection, however crass, of Indian middle-class values, is rife with instances of the family cold shoulder when male children fail to arrive. We have doctors using sex-detection techniques to aid and abet foeticide. Nip the female in the bud.

The *Brihadaranyaka Upanishad* is a veritable honeycomb. Much honey flows, much sweet food for thought. But with this emerge clouds of bees buzzing in our ancestral bonnets. I can almost hear an angry hum from protesting bastions of male indignation. Our suitors, our protectors, our mates, our near, dear and caring ones will deny themselves blue in their hurt faces or even ask forlornly if they are not different. But I maintain that deep within, buried out of sight and mind, pulsates quietly a racial memory of injustices meted out in thought, word and deed.

Modern life, its compulsions, its exigencies are perhaps doing away with the word and partially, the deed in the urban, educated, city professional. Hence the lip service, the acceptance of feminist outcries, the seeming accommodation. But in thought, the old seed is firmly lodged, waiting to sprout whenever and wherever conditions are conducive.

To get back to the rite. There is a cold, clinical approach that sets the tone. The object is spelt out clearly—to beget a son to specifications. The procedure is then laid down, step by step. First, the approach to the woman. Set about acquiring your partner's cooperation in the following manner, advises the instructor. Attract her, persuade her with blandishments. If that doesn't work, lure her with gifts and ornaments. If she is still not willing, beat her with your hands—and here, aggression mounts—or with a stick. Of course, if she fails to conceive, the fault is hers. And the punishment? A quick threat of a rite to deprive her of her trump card, her fertility.

On this victorious note, the man presumably enters *grihastashrama,* the life of a householder, the second of the four stages of life. There is domestic harmony, all dissidence successfully eliminated. The woman submits with grace or without, adopts his life-aims, the most obsessive and persistent of which is the performance of the funeral rites. This being an all-important job, replete with power over life and death, is a wholly male preserve, hence the son. And back we are, circling, to square one, in this case, the rites for a special kind of son, custom-made to suit individual preferences. The text goes on to specify the various rituals—for a fair son, a tawny, brown son, a dark, red-eyed son, a pedagogue, an orator, a conqueror. ...

There is a loophole, a tiny one, provided. In the unlikely event of your wanting a daughter, there is a special ritual. You are also expected to want only one kind of daughter, a *pundita,* a pedagogue. No other model is mentioned. This stray, inconsequential thought wanders into the elaborate structure of ritual for a dream-son, a bit of fluff that the text blows away.

The Brihadaranyaka, of course, provides its own counters to this one-sided approach to life and gender. Gargi was the woman philosopher who cross-examined the redoubtable Yajnavalkya when he laid almost unchallenged claim to knowledge of the Absolute. She prevented this humiliating walkover, chided the meek, cowed down assembly of male scholars and provoked them into putting up a respectable resistance.

The wise men rose to the occasion feebly, each subsiding after a couple of questions which Yajnavalkya shot down with insulting ease. Then Gargi entered the fray. She asked nine questions, stretching Yajnavalkya's communicating skills to near-breaking point, temporarily gave in to his threat of causing her inquisitive head to fall off, but recovered to ask on. And she did not do so timidly. "Prepare yourself", she said, with a great surge of confidence. She announced her intention to let fly two more arrows from her superior bowstring, drawn with consummate skill and expertise. There is all the excitement of a duel that, won or lost, would do her credit. As a matter of fact, she lost; only to go down in tradition as a model for thinkers.

No less in stature was the wise, though less fiery Maitreyi, one of Yajnavalkya's two wives, the other being Katyayani. The sage declared his intention to renounce the world and before departing, to divide his worldly possessions. Katyayani took her share willingly. Maitreyi however, turned round and asked him: "Will all your wealth make me immortal?" "Certainly not," replied Yajnavalkya; whereupon, with the clarity and discernment of true wisdom, Maitreyi said to her husband, "Tell me that which you know". She was richly rewarded, not only with the instruction that followed but with his loving response. "You were dear to me, Maitreyi, but now you are even dearer."

We are familiar with the 'better' and blind to the 'worse' in our culture. The glories, the heights, the wisdom, the insights, the reach of Indian philosophy have been lauded time and time again. But the picture of everyday realities it paints, the pragmatics it has worked out, the daily manoeuvre, the manipulation, the power games it has played so skilfully with sex and governance and social norms have not been looked at honestly by succeeding generations. We must know the whole truth about ourselves. In ruthless self-analysis lies the key to progress. Once the true picture is drawn, we can proceed to re-draw it.

Reviewing and jettisoning is ancient Indian methodology. That is what the Upanishads are all about. The Vedas were reviewed by the Upanishadic seers. The speculations that questioned, and at times toppled, entrenched practices and beliefs, are amongst our greatest treasures. Their failures are ours to rectify, their loop-holes ours to plug; their insights ours to continue, their modes of behaviour ours to modify and adopt. *Kala*, time, is of the essence. We do not have to adhere to the letter of the law of traditions, we must emulate its spirit; the resilience, the flexibility, the agility, the hunger for excellence, the relentless pursuit of truth.

We have much to emulate, much to reject, but first we must see ourselves, not with a borrowed vision, but with our own. This applies particularly poignantly to our struggles on the feminist front. We must not be distracted by our glories, our exotics, our dramatics. There is a preen in the Indian woman's step, a hint of a peacock-strut. A symbol of relative stability, we are particularly vulnerable and open to complacency. Our colourful, flowing clothes don't help; they have turned into costumes, and we, actors in a costume drama. Our projections abroad are in the nature of displays. And amidst all the sound and clamour of our glorious past and colourful present, the voices of protest, the notes of warning get drowned.

Gargi fought to the finish and submitted not to intimidation but to evidence of truth; Maitreyi refused to be side-tracked or to settle for less. True, these were exceptional women confronting an exceptional man. But the pursuit of excellence is a matter of choosing the right models and fixing targets. And persistence. We need to resuscitate our Gargis and our Maitreyis.

The Tree in India, Myth and Symbol

The Vedas speak through branch and twig
of this little jackfruit tree
the rest is Shiva all of it
each leaf, each fruit, each section of each fruit
is like a lingam, Shiva's sign
so too the seeds enclosed within
shaped like Shivalingams all
the sap that rises in this tree
to cover it with tender shoots
is Shiva, so let's worship him.

— Rasappa Kavi Rayar

The trees of India stand tall in the sap of centuries. It flows rich and full in their veins as symbol, myth and legend. The wisdom and the folly, the sense, the nonsense and the commonsense that is India lie as much in her tree-lore as in her great systems of philosophy or metaphysics. For India lives at many levels.

In India, more than anywhere else, the tree is much more than just a tree. It bears a load of symbols and the weight of an ancient religious tradition that was born and bred in her many forests. The Indian way of penetrating to the heart of any matter has always been through the symbol. India is a great seeker, as she is a great story-teller. The search is all; the symbol, and whatever tale happens to hang thereby is a proven instrument in that search. Hence the welter of myth. Again, the symbol is closely linked with the Indian concept of *maya*, the powerful veil of illusion. Is a spade really a spade? Softening a hard fact into a symbol, a resilient, absorbent and plastic medium for truth, is one of India's great talents. It also serves as a concomitant to the question of existence as *maya*.

As a consequence, the Indian mind shifts from fact to illusion to reality to truth, adeptly side-stepping life's pitfalls and journeying through to its destined end. And all the while we keep a tight hold on reality—and the symbol. The Indian literally 'senses' an object till it begins to stand for more than itself and becomes a morsel of experience, a symbol, in fact.

Once perceived, the symbol leads past itself through layers of meaning to fresh insights. And if this process is a collective, continuing, racial habit of mind, we have symbols that grow and link into feasible systems of life and thought. As they have in India. A way out of the *maya* of it all.

For it is through 'symbolic' cogitation that the Indian has hit upon yet another common Indian activity—transcendence. A symbol, by definition, transcends the concrete. And there is little denying that life is largely a matter of confronting and then transcending the so-called concrete realities. Much of Indian escapism is nothing but transcendence.

And now we come to one of our most enduring and beloved symbols, the tree. It grows through the myth and legend of India, taking root in the Indian consciousness, shading its great visions, guarding its buried treasures of thought and feeling. A tropical profusion of ideas clings to this symbol—superstition, magic, necromancy, hidden fears, horrors, joy, sorrow, contentment, enlightenment, sheer poetry—for it has been a long and eventful time in the making.

To begin at the beginning is to begin with the forest—the natural habitat of the tree. Many of our guidelines for living, our speculations, enlightened or otherwise, have come out of forest workshops and seminars on Truth which led to the findings of the *Brahmanas,* the *Aranyakas,* the *Upanishads.* Much of our teaching was done in forests by sages who ran exclusive schools away from the distractions of town and city or even home. The first of the four stages of life, *brahmacharya,* the intensive learning stage, was ideally passed in a hermitage. The third and fourth stages, retirement *(vanaprastha)* and withdrawal *(sannyasa)* also took one to the forest. The forest then, was almost an institution, a formalised training ground for life, here and hereafter. It was a veritable school for symbols.

Our epics celebrate forest life even when it is a part of exile, as in the epic *Ramayana*. Chitrakoota and Panchavati, the forest homes of the exiled Prince Rama and his wife Sita, symbolise conjugal bliss, the *parnakuti* (leaf-hut) being the ideal home of the ideal couple. The *Puranas* talk of creating a *panchavati* in one's private garden with the planting of five (*pancha*) trees—the *peepul*, the banyan, the *bilva*, the *amalaka* and the *ashoka*. This is how the Indian lives out his symbols.

The forest is a living, pulsing presence. In the epic *Ramayana,* the first encounter the god-prince Rama had with evil was through the female demon, Tataka. Her mere presence had laid waste large tracts; the evil in her had sucked the life out of her environment. Then Rama arrives, she is killed and the forest comes alive in a burst of smiling relief and blossom. Happiness, Valmiki seems to say, is a forest in flower and, of course, the forest is never just a forest. The personification and symbolism are vivid and unmistakable. Again, Sugriva describing his brother Vali's prowess to Rama, trembling at the very thought, recounts how Vali had only to stride past for the mighty *sala* trees to shed their leaves in fright. Man and nature interacted with an intimacy that spoke of a close and bonded relationship.

From forest to grove, park, garden and avenue was a natural progression. The taming of wild nature into more companionable forms gave rise to fresh symbols. Planting and conservation became acts of duty and charity enjoined by the *shastras* (rule books). Rite and ritual took over. According to the texts of the *Agni Purana*, a conservation rite becomes a soul-saving act and the trees themselves objects of veneration, appeasement and invocation. There is also a detailed description of a model garden, giving positions of specific trees, shrubs and an adjoining flower garden. A household garden, true, but explicitly ritualistic in concept. The forest has been brought home and familiarity was turning trees and plants into presences with human demands, useful presences at that. They were beginning to wear their symbols with an air of noble ease. Close proximity, perhaps, magnified and made tangible their needs in the eye of the beholder.

Trees now began to acquire a personality, an aura and an area of power and influence, and inevitably, divine patronage. Temples had *sthalavrikshas,* trees connected with their installation. Trees were being draped, in other words, with increasing symbolic significance.

And here the legends and mythology begin. Pressed between the pages of history and pre-history, our trees speak of a sylvan past, peopled by spirits, demons and deities as they frolic, sport and preside over votive or festive rites. Mallinatha, commenting on a verse in Kalidasa's *Malavikagnimitra,* lists ten trees and their longings while waiting to burst into bloom. Each one demands a different cajolement from a young and beautiful woman before it gives birth, that is, flowers. The *priyangu* craves a touch, the *bakula,* thirsts for a mouthful of wine, the *ashoka* a kick, the *tilaka* a glance, the *kurabaka* an embrace. The *mandara* longs for soft speech, the *champa* for a sweet, provocative smile. The mango wishes to be blown upon, the *nameru* favours song and the *karnikara,* dance. The general symbolism is clear—youth, beauty, love, awakening, fertilisation, fecundity. But the caring individuation speaks of intimacy and a deep-seated conviction that man and nature stem from one source, one elemental, undifferentiated substance.

The myths of creation, of which there are many, pinpoint the place of trees in nature's hierarchy. According to the *Bhagavata Purana,* the trees are the first among Brahma-Prajapati's creations. In another version, in the *Shatapatha Brahmana,* the Creator having created Agni, fire, feared for his own life. He rubbed his palms together and produced butter as an offering, saying, 'Drink, as you burn.' It was this rite that produced trees, plants and herbs. In both myths, trees acquire symbolic significance. In the first, they assume chronological pride of place, and in the second, they are an answer to the Creator's prayer, no less! The tree is beginning to acquire an august lineage with divine connections.

There are two motifs that the tree in India is inextricably linked with—water and the serpent. In a creation myth in *Matsya Purana,* the wandering, ageless sage, Markandeya, comes upon an infant on a banyan leaf, then a boy under a banyan tree in a vast sea. The child is the Primeval Being, Narayana, *Purusha* (Male) who rests on the waters of being, on the coiled serpent Sesha, the stuff of life. An early Buddhist legend about the Buddha's enlightenment has the same symbolic syndrome. In a dramatic account, ten thousand worlds resounded with thunder when he saw the light. He sat for seven days under a peepul, then moved on for another seven days to a banyan, and lastly to the tree of the Serpent King. In the moist recesses of its roots lived the cobra king, Muchalinda, who sheltered the Buddha from a raging storm with his outspread hood. When Buddha emerged from his trance, Muchalinda stood, hands folded in worship, transformed into a gentle youth, ready to receive instruction.

Another mystic episode establishes the serpent-water linkage. Balarama, elder brother and companion-incarnation with Krishna, was considered to be actually an incarnation of Sesha. His end comes as he sits lost in thought on the seashore at Dwaraka. A serpent, his real self, crawls out of his mouth and into the ocean and rejoins the formless abyss, the waters of life.

In Karnataka, sculpted serpent-stones (*nagakals*) are left immersed by the image-maker in water for six months—a symbolic entry of water as the life-giving element. They are then set up under a peepul or a banyan for regular worship. In Kerala, sacred groves called *kavus* are set apart for snakes. The practice supposedly started with Parashurama, an incarnation of Vishnu and legendary founder of Kerala. It was a measure intended to keep the inhabited areas clear of snakes for the original settlers.

From representing an undifferentiated, informing force, trees began to stand for separate powers, spirits, demons, deities. The forests of Buddhist legend are full of chatty tree spirits, *yakshas* and *yakshis,* busily managing the lives of their fellow-beings. In Vedic and in Upanishadic times, priests and sages transmuted their forest experiences into symbols—ritualistic at first, and later, speculative. The bank of symbols was growing.

An account of just two of our major tree symbols makes a gripping chronicle of times and places past, modes of thought and feeling now merely vestigial. Yet they are reminders of a living symbolic presence on many ceremonial occasions today; house-warming ceremonies, marriages, festivals, funerals. For the Vedic chant, *shruti* (that which is revealed), and other forms of the oral tradition, will prevail. The Indian way of life bonds you with its myth and legend.

The first among trees is the *ashwattha,* the Bo Tree, or the peepul. There is no way of challenging or disputing this. The Buddha saw the light under it. The god Krishna, in the *Bhagvad Gita* speaks of it in laudatory terms. First, in Chapter 10, in the midst of a torrential flow of stunning metaphors that establish his lineage and cosmic stature, he refers to himself as the '*ashwattha* among trees'. In an equally unforgettable series of five verses in Chapter 15, he designates the peepul as the cosmic Tree of Life. It spreads beyond sight and knowledge, both above and below, baffling in its mystic inversion, with roots above and branches below; only the axe of detachment can cut through to the roots of this mystery of mysteries. In these verses, symbols are hoisted on to every part of the peepul by the Lord. The leaves are the

Vedas, and so on till the whole of Creation and Causation sits firmly perched on it, ensconced forever. It is an elaborate metaphor and coming from the Cosmic Hero himself, not to be taken lightly.

The *ashwattha* or the peepul as master-symbol attracts scores of associations. Jyeshtha, elder sister of Lakshmi and bringer of bad luck, resides in the peepul; hence it is only to be touched on Saturdays when Lakshmi comes visiting her, it is recommended. Else, bad luck dogs you. Vaishnavi, female energy of Vishnu, one of the Saptamatrikas (seven mothers) sits under it. It features as an object of worship on a Mohenjodaro seal. In the *Atharva Veda*, the peepul is used in a rite to ensure a male child. The peepul is an aggressive, virile, male image—naturally, since it is symbolic of the Cosmic Purusha (Male). It is used, therefore, in battle rites, where its fierce, destructive and hostile powers are evoked. The *ashwattha* grows into other trees, uniting, penetrating, destroying. One can see both the sexual and the conquering elements that are associated with this tree of trees. In the *Chandogya Upanishad*, it is the focus of the sun's rays and therefore, of knowledge, light and time— the sun being the source of all these. It is believed to shower *soma*—the joy, the abundance, the elixir of life, the nectar of the gods. The heavenly *ashwattha* has *soma* growing under it.

The *ashwattha* is indeed the prime Indian tree-symbol. In comparison, the fabled *kalpataru*, Indra's wish-fulfilling tree, seems a jewelled artifice. Every village has a peepul as the centre of its social and religious activities. The Indian consciousness has invested it with values that open secret doors and lay bare the treasures of Indian thought. It is a tree that takes this heavy load with the graceful forbearance of an enlightened soul, the Indian goal and ideal. No concept seems too large or abstract and equally, no idea or fancy or even whim, too small or trite for it to receive. That in itself symbolises a basic Indian attitude, acceptance— very often mistakenly construed as resignation. To receive is to absorb, to grow. It is a positive act, as productive as the peepul, strong support of Indian life.

Coming a close second in importance is the ubiquitous banyan. Its aura is one of majesty and extent. Its aerial roots are its own regenerative as well as destructive force, as it spreads and acquires fresh territory. It stands for death not as finality but as renewal in the on-going cosmic process. In the *Matsya Purana* it bore the Primal Being as the prophetic babe on its leaf, floating on the waters of life. The *Chandogya Upanishad* gives it the authority of privileged speculation. In a famous dialogue between Svetaketu, the avid student and his wise teacher-father, Svetaketu is asked to bring a banyan fruit. "Split it," said the father, and then, "what do you see?" "Miniscule seeds," replied Svetaketu. "Break a seed", instructed his father, ordering a second scrutiny. "I see nothing", reported the son. "That which you do not see, is the *sat,* the essence," declared the father. "The whole huge tree grew out of that *sat.* You are that, Svetaketu." "You are that" (*tat tvam asi*) has acquired the status of a mantra; and *"tat tvam"* has coalesced to form *'tattvam'* the word for principle/ essence/truth.

The banyan has its deities too. Aiyanar is one of our more esoteric gods. He is, in parts of South India, the guardian deity of the village and sits under the banyan tree. Dakshinamurthi, the aspect of Siva as teacher, communicates the truth silently to his pupils, seated under the banyan tree of knowledge. It was under a banyan that Satyavan died and his wife Savitri began her famed argument with death, at the end of which she emerged triumphant and won her husband his life.

There are too many trees and too many stories to even list here, but mention must be made of the *sala* and the *ashoka*. The Buddha was born as his mother, Maya Devi, stood holding the branch of a flowering *sala* tree in the Lumbini grove. And she dreamt of his coming under an *ashoka*. The *ashoka* has associations both secular and sacred. It is one of the five flower arrows of Madana, the God of Love. *Vasanta* (Spring), his inseparable companion, appears dressed in *ashoka* leaves. Sita sat out her prison term in Lanka in an *ashoka* grove: and the tree flowers only when kicked by a beautiful woman. The symbolism is remarkably consistent—spring, love, beauty, women and fertility. The *ashoka* blooms as an enduring symbol of rejuvenation.

Myth and symbol twine round our trees like flowering creepers and the stories spread their fragrance down the years. The emotions evoked by these cover the whole spectrum of human experience—and the symbol survives. The grove remains the Indian ideal of peace, the forest a spiritual refuge. Eroded soil and values or denuded forests cannot wholly diminish the strength of this abiding symbol.

THE STORY SPREADS

......by word of mouth, largely. The oral tradition lends itself easily to the spreading of myth through our fine and performing arts, both folk and classical. Poetry and song burst into flame, sparked by the magic of living myth. Indian thought spreads because it both grips and fascinates.

Sway in your hands the deer and the flame
swings on your head the crescent moon
in and out of your hair the Ganga at play
dancing, dancing, keeping time
Shivakami moves in rhythm true
Brahma too, and all the gods
Ganesha with his elephant head
Murugan joins, the little one
dancing, dancing, here they come
Indra and the eighteen sages
guardians of the eight directions
sacred flowers and sacred grass
thrill and tremble with delight
watching Shiva's bull step high
dancing, dancing, one and all
thus with all your retinue
in all your glory, all your pomp
Tillai Shivan, Shivakami's love, lord of my heart
come to meet your creature, me.

—unknown

The Festival of India in America

*

It was 3 June 1985 and I was on the 9.30 a.m. Amtrak to Washington. The train did its customary quickslide out of Penn Station in New York and I slipped into my comfortable seat. I was a bag of mixed feelings with a Granny Smith in my hand—a flawless, smooth, juicy green apple. It was exactly like at least a dozen others I had consumed during my month-long stay in the States. It held no surprises. I thought fondly of its counterpart back home and the wildly fluctuating quality from apple to apple, sometimes from bite to bite!

I had over three hours to think as I looked out and watched the weather, all forecast and dripping, come true. I felt wise, old and excited, all at the same time. Full of pride, too, for India—full of the joy of being led by the world's most youthful Prime Minister who would, in a fortnight, take the American public by storm with what, I was sure, would be an outstanding performance—I had just had my anticipations confirmed as I watched a direct telecast over Indian television. And my cultural nose was twitching with anticipation at the thought of catching two Indian exhibitions—one, the sculpture show at the National Galley of Art which had already opened on 13 May and the other to open the next day, 4 June—*Aditi, a celebration of life* as its title proclaimed, at the Natural History Museum of the Smithsonian, Washington D.C.

Off the main lobby to the right one encountered the usual splash of *shamiana* colours and a shop full of Indian handicrafts which even when shoddy, make, I think, the world's most interesting shopping. And these, I was relieved to note, had been carefully screened for quality. Already the shop had turned into a bustling bazaar, minutes after the museum doors had opened to let the day's crowds in. One escalator level down, you entered Aditi. It felt, quite aptly, womb-like; a guha, a cavern. With the public opening an hour away, life at Aditi was just beginning to stir into celebration.

As I wound my way through a totally transformed American museum interior, I suspended disbelief with the greatest ease. I was in India. Most of the artefacts were in place—old along with new, in the wonder that is the continuity of India. It was high design with great restraint and displaying a creative ability that took my breath away. Showcase and gallery seemed to merge with tiled courtyard, rich bedchamber and street-theatre with little trace of posturing.

And it was live, truly so. As one inspected objects of art and craft, the culture that breathed life into them literally awakened around you. The diminutive *baul* singer from Bengal, Phulmala Dasi, sang out in ringing tones her mystic strains, strumming on her ektara—"O, dark one, I call out but you do not hear, you who sped to Draupadi in her hour of distress ...". I walked down a narrow alley and turning a corner caught sight of Jivya Soma the celebrated Warli tribal painter doing a wall-painting. I had produced a book on his work and written out the legends that each one told. His simple, elemental face lit up with recognition and we conversed briefly, he in broken Hindi and I in broken Marathi, and I recovered totally from long and efficient store aisles where all you met were price tags and consumer over-choice.

I bumped, literally, into the bahurupiya, (assumer of many roles) who did his dual act, merely flicking a veil to change it—one side of his face old and toothless and wrinkled with the matted white hair of poverty-stricken old age. He croaked and gurgled and begged and I saw the collecting groups draw back, startled with the street-realities of India. This was neither the romanticised, bleeding-heart, distanced versions of cinema and news media, nor the India of research-foundation studies, seminars and workshops poring solemnly over their projects, fact-finding and summing up. Here was a genuine jhalak, a flash, of truth by one who experienced it unvarnished, and unselfconsciously made it part of his act, his repertoire.

As the bahurupiya passed on, I entered the courtyard of the wedding theme. The 'horse-man' trotted around and sang, full-throated, first a song of the bride dreaming of gota (tinsel) on her veil, on her blouse, on her skirt. He etched before you the onrush of a bridal mood—the child bride, her head full of the finery to come, only barely sensing the solemnity of it all. The next song set her in her new home; she pleaded with her mother-in-law. "*Saasu*, handle your son—he tails me incessantly. He breaks my pot, just as I have finished drawing water. He picks up and scatters the flour just as I have finished grinding my wheat, and when I am cooking my *rotis*, he breaks my earthen stove with the iron blower."

I had had enough of bride-burning and stereotyped mothers-in-law and unfeeling bridegrooms. Here was the authentic tradition—a human, humane situation where two women linked in spontaneous rapport, as boy chased girl with love and joy. All is not burning and rotten in the state of India, dear reporter! I found myself translating to an eager by-stander who could get nowhere near the young volunteer-translator. She, in any case, stood uneasy and inadequate, trying to form a bridge between performer and questioner. Obviously the rush of opening had overlooked proper testing and screening. I hoped these things would iron out as the show progressed.

I moved on to the infant and child section passing 'expectant motherhood' celebrating new life about to resume its cycle of birth and death. Weaving like a leitmotif through it all, one met the aged teacher-pilgrim on the back of his young and faithful disciple. "These days", he sang and spoke, "children do not obey their parents; but my beloved *chela* (pupil) bears me on his back to Kashi, Badrinath and Hardwar. Hurry, child, it's late. Life is a bubble of water." This was the wisdom of Indian philosophy which permeates the humblest and most illiterate of its sons and daughters; which is what helps one bear up, which is what the fact-finders miss. I am not justifying the poverty or disease. I am only underlining the strength of the Indian psyche that we all draw upon when the ills and afflictions of life overtake us. I feel prayerful about this strength and fear for it, but hope that the influential minority will identify it and reinforce it without embarrassment in the face of rapid high-tech advance. We are unique and we should continue to be so.

I went round in circles, changing direction, reading the connecting blurbs, watching the performers slipping into their act with ease, chatting to them. Infancy, through maturity and old age, back and forth—there was an entry point and exit point but within those bounds you could trace and re-trace your steps. It was cyclical; no arrows, no direction, not over-streamlined. This did create some confusion for the American public for whom life was a linear progression with a beginning, a middle and an end, for they believe, "we shall pass this way but once". But for me, the maze, the unstructured circular order, the continuity and the bewilderment broke the ordered schedule of a normal museum show. There were inter-spaces for ritual and ceremony, work and play— *mehndi* on the hands, embroidery on the veil, mobiles on the rocking cradle, icons for worship, fun-fairs and temple visits—a whole illusory, but living world of beauty, art and life in the raw.

I made my final exit flanked by giant terracotta horses, guardians of village welfare, acts of faith.

Palaniappan, the craftsman, spoke to me eagerly in Tamil, as did the Tanjore and Mysore glass painters who worked, like all the other craftsmen, with quiet industry. I had started out with, and still have reservations on this whole idea of India performing abroad, in order to impress, particularly at what must have been immense expense. I still believe in a continuous flow of 'projection' for our image. I feel, perhaps with the arrogance of an ancient civilisation that has managed to continue, not fizzle out or freeze, that the world should come and get us, that we should not have to, in cultural terms, show off, but be revealed. And if there has to be a showing, it should be at the request and expense of the host country. After all, we are on show right here, for the seeker; on site—heat, dust, discomfort and all. But having seen Aditi, there seems to be a case for displaying ourselves and our finer points; our wisdom, our strength, our beauty, our depth, our formidable craft resources, our skills, to the unaware public of a nation like America.

America is big, new and thrusting, wide open and receptive and eager to get it. This opening cultural gambit gave it to them comprehensively, compactly, easefully and in superb taste. I saw a fairly blasé crowd trickle in, thicken, and transform before my very eyes into the kind of curious, interested and totally involved groups that collect round an Indian bazaar or street show. They were amused, entertained, informed and madly interested. That mollified me somewhat.

Shiva in Philadelphia

From time to time, as the need arises, or as the fancy takes him, Shiva steps out from Kailasa to visit and even take up, as only Indian Gods can, parallel, simultaneous residence in a city of his choice. So it was that he entered Madurai, in the form of Sundareswara, the beautiful bridegroom, to wed Minakshi, the Pandyan princess; whereby hangs, as we all know, a legend and a temple.

So again, in Chidambaram, in Tanjore, in the golden hall of Tillai, he stages for all eternity the cosmic dance, his left foot raised in the inaugural step that launches the drumbeat of life, its mystic rhythms. And in the spring of 1981, he manifested himself in the city of Philadelphia; in gracious response to a concerted act of devoted scholarship that paid homage to him in the best traditions of American research.

'The Manifestations of Shiva' exhibition, part of a year-long focus on the complexities of Indian culture moved to Seattle and then to Los Angeles from Philadelphia before the exhibits, paintings, sculptures and bronzes retired to their appointed niches in, mainly, American homes and museums. Enhancing the exhibition and reinforcing it was an on-going and varied backdrop of cultural events that brought home to viewers the full force of this complex member of the Hindu triad of gods.

Viewers filed past a graphic trident composed in stark ivory and austere brown, up a flight of stairs to a plinth-level hall to pass under a tall doorway announcing 'Shiva' on a glowing vermillion square evocative of his consort, Devi. The build-up of the Shiva mood was complete. The pilgrimage began and the picture gallery funneled you into the hidden recesses of the Shiva mystique. Shiva as *Lingodbhava* manifest in his own creative phallic symbol, Shiva as Nataraja, lord of dance, Shiva as Gangadhara receiving and reducing to a drop the turbulent, arrogant abundance of the river Ganga as she throws her divine tantrum and threatens to flood the world, Shiva as Bhairava, Shiva with Parvati and sons in domestic and conjugal scenes almost placidly mundane, except for Shivaesque twists—stringing skulls handed over to him by attentive children, quaffing intoxicants offered to him by a doting Parvati, Shiva and Parvati taking a mountainous path down to earth hand in hand, bag and baggage, sons mounted as parents step carefully over craggy, precipitous ledges. Shiva as the painter fixed him in settings familiar to him, Shiva as he lived in the hearts of gifted men who saw him through their own veils of love and devotion, personalised presentations that drew the God into the charmed circle of a personal vision.

Leaving the intimate and private world of paintings that called for attention to fascinating minutiae, one walked into the more dramatic large-scale world of metal and stone sculpture, representing every well-known school and provenance—Gupta, Chola, Pala, Hoysala, Rajasthan, Central India, Tamil Nadu, Karnataka. A few smaller bronzes scaled down the perception once more, at journey's end, to manageable handling of the impact of Shiva.

Right through, the concise, succinct captions attached to the exhibits formed a running commentary building up historically and anecdotally, the legend of Shiva. For those who needed more elucidation, there was a portable hand-audio set with a well-scripted and simple tale of Shiva, at pre-determined points. The pilgrims progressed on a programmed, charted course on the highway to Shiva.

In the auditorium that afternoon was organised a South Indian music concert of Shiva songs, partly played on the flute and partly sung. The flute was not a happy choice of instrument, for its sweet seductiveness went ill with the fire and ice of Shiva and was, besides, too strongly reminiscent of Venugopala Krishna who stole the hearts of the milkmaids of Brindavan. Sweet heartbreak was hardly the right note to strike for Shiva, the destroyer of Kama—Shiva, whose love-making is as much terror as ecstasy.

I walked away after five hours spent with Shiva, savouring the intensity of an Indian experience abroad. The late afternoon sun set golden fire to the honey-coloured, columned structure of the Philadelphia Museum of Art, lending support to the popular belief that the golden hall of Tillai is indeed the human heart which rises above time and place when it tunes in to the beat of Shiva, Nataraja.

Transpersonal Encounters

The International Transpersonal Association conferred in Bombay in 1982 to thrash out publicly and formally a growing conviction that the spirit of science and the science of spirituality explore the same field—the field of human and cosmic consciousness. These two activities, for many centuries in the West, as well as in cultures dominated by the West, have been proceeding in a mutually exclusive manner. Scientific rationality, in this process, has had to reject, even denounce the insights of spirituality. Mysticism, vision and revelation were seen as obstacles in the path of scientific investigation.

The wheel is turning. Scientists working on matter and the concrete have been left holding the abstract and staring into cosmic space. They are witnesses, suddenly, to the same inner spectacles that the opposition, the spiritual camp, most persistently in the East, have been going on about. In fact they are beginning to see—and believe—that there is only one spectacle, the inner one.

And that it is inner-most when it is outer-most. This, as the opening address by Dr. Grof confirmed, is the case for transpersonality—crossing and going beyond the ego and the limited personality into the undivided, unifying cosmic consciousness.

The conference opened with a Sanskrit prayer chanted beautifully; a bold and effective shortcut to the spiritual stance necessary for such a meeting. A get-set-go shattered briefly and quite unnecessarily by a clapping audience. Prayer is a joint-venture into a mood—not a performance.

I picked on two people initially for a brief and specific entry into the transpersonal spirit because of their vocations—Fritjof Capra, physicist and Frances Vaughan, psychotherapist. Talking to these two persons, one dealing with the science of matter and the other the science of personality, would cover much ground surely.

Fritjof Capra, young and certain after his ordeal of uncertainty as a scientist, hippie and seeker, spoke of the inevitability of spirituality which, mainly because of the accident of birth, I had never even questioned. He linked it with ecology.

"My world view is ecological, the environment is a path to spirituality. My way lies through that".

"How do you in practice keep your lines open, your contact with the spirit alive?" I asked.

Fritjof hesitated.

"These examples might sound absurd, but they help, they are important. I drive a small car, where most Americans drive limousines—that is, if I must. I walk most of the time, or cycle. I take a shopping bag, I avoid supermarkets ...".

I couldn't help smiling.

"You see, the wastefulness of bringing home shopping in a surfeit of paper bags, even that is a blow to ecology, in a way, as significant as an electric lawn-mower ...".

"Or an electric can-opener, which is worse," I put in, recounting my response to this gadget when I first encountered it. It stood between me and the simple act of opening a can as surely as the electric mower fouls up a straightforward contact with nature. His next statement was vehement.

"I never use cans or processed foods. I cook".

I saw the connection. Every convenience, every package, every facility is a step away from yourself. The modern exercise in spirituality must at least partly consist in reducing these and renewing links with the spirit. The path to this truth must be as difficult, exciting and compelling for Fritjof Capra as his path along particle physics. And the dawning realization that the two are really one.

We discussed the need for rite and ritual.

"We in India have a glut of religious props and beliefs which we can and do draw upon. What about you?"

"We have none. We try and bring ritual into our lives. I keep a Chinese Book of Changes and treat it with reverence, make a rite of it. I remember a Japanese woman executive I dealt with. She used to arrive, svelte and Western, dressed in a business suit. When I met her in Japan and she put me through the ceremonial paces dressed in a kimono at a traditional Japanese inn, I was amazed at the transformation."

I pointed out that to her the business meeting must have been an equally serious rite performed meticulously. That is the strength of the Oriental. She felt no dichotomy.

With his faith in traditional cultures, we just had to discuss Indian godmen and gurus.

"They have to develop the right symbols for us. Either they dilute it for our consumption or invalidate our context." He took a well-known name.

"He understood me and my ecology but when I tried to relate spirituality to economics and politics, he turned away".

I understood. Spirituality was ancient and Eastern, the rest modern and Western. Spirituality has become the preserve of the withdrawn, not a part of life as it must and should be. The transpersonal perspective, if it worked, could do just that.

"I have found a guru. My senior colleague. I don't talk about it. But he is just that."

He had also found a temple he wanted to see. He was wavering—the Mahalakshmi or Babulnath? I recommended Babulnath. Physics seemed a more Shaivite subject.

The transpersonal mantle sat more easily on Frances Vaughan. The psyche and the human consciousness has more room for the spirit.

"We go beyond the ego and draw heavily on cross-cultural and inter-disciplinary methods."

How advanced was transpersonal psychology? "It is taught formally in many universities. I myself, apart from my clinical practice, teach at the California Institute of Transpersonal Psychology and edit their official journal. The whole thing hinges on the premise that the personality operates or could and should operate, at five levels—physical, mental, emotional, spiritual and community. We need to go far. We are only a decade old."

I asked her too about rites and rituals. "We need to create them. For instance, our transpersonal fraternity joins hands and observes silence before a meal. The silence is an individual experience but also a collective binding gesture."

"What will you do with a generation that comes looking for a belief system or faith and doesn't know where to find it. What is your action line?"

"We offer courses in many belief systems, programmed by experts at the Institute. They familiarise themselves with what is offered and come to their own choices and conclusions."

There is a whole growing body of transpersonal literature. Frances Vaughan mentioned Ken Wilber.

"We use his books as texts. He doesn't lecture—only writes; and has contributed significantly to the transpersonal perspective."

She answered my last question, while it was still half-raised.

"We have no charismatic leader and personality dominating the transpersonal scene. It is an easy association of like-minded people. But we see the need for spirituality as an urgent and compelling one."

India, target of speedy, spectacular cults and prime producer of godmen with foreign followings, needs an assurance like this, particularly from America. We have EST which comes down on itself with a heavy hand and a bludgeon of destruction which Shiva might just manage to handle right; lion-tamer trainers who claim to deliver the goods—and at the same time disclaim the existence of any goods to deliver with their crash courses in nothing-something-everything, who plough through lives heedlessly, and at times, dangerously. In comparison, these 'messiahs' came with a gentle, clear and undeniable message and wide open minds, waiting for people to absorb and accept in their own time and at their own pace. One could not help wishing them luck.

After a preliminary sampling of transpersonality, I wished the Conference and its participants luck, only in a manner of speaking. The next week, after a fairly full participation in their sessions, I reiterated my wish because I think they really needed it. Not because they did not have a point but because I questioned the ardour and naivety of their infant hopes.

The still, small voice of the spirit is something the mystics have always strained to hear and the modern scientist, to hush. Today, science and spirituality make strange, but inevitable bed-fellows. International Transpersonal conferences are held to make the world adjust to this partnership.

The transpersonal fraternity had aired their views week-long, using many voices to convey their message— Tai Chi, Shamanism, Jewish, Christian, Islamic, Hindu and Buddhist mysticism. All these age-old explorations of the human consciousness had been mined for spiritual resources to reinforce almost every field of modern science and take it forwards on a transformative, transpersonal path. For that way seemed to lie salvation.

The Transpersonal Conference was a study in persuasiveness. All missions are. But quite commendably, the structure of the conference allowed for free movement of your interest and attention from presentation to presentation, taking or leaving at will.

I took mainly the Western presenters. For what interested me was the impact of ancient Indian wisdom on modern Western scientists. It had obviously sent them reeling. They were looking back in time and outwards into space with great regret. They were searching not only their own traditions for renewed links with the spirit but were scouring the world, particularly India, for aids to integration.

The search is frantic and at times absurd. The findings, exciting to the novice discoverer, need to be handled with care. Let me illustrate.

Dr. Malcolm Carruthers and Dr. Vera Carruthers, among the more convincing and persuasive voices of transpersonality, advocate and practise Autogenic Therapy. Carefully programmed sessions used taped mantras, meditational processes and 'paint-out' therapy for Creative Mobilisation. It was flattering to hear them praise the yoganauts of the East and pity the cosmonauts of the West who return from the Sea of Tranquility on the moon to a sea of tranquillisers on earth.

Their personalities, he, quietly and forcefully charismatic and she, pleasantly intoning as though all the world were a bedside and she the ideal manner, nearly did the trick. I almost bought it all; till a sample process was tried out on the audience. With eyes closed we followed Vera's brisk, hearty instructions to 'still the mind' and think of nothing. At least it taught me one lesson, all over again. Never sit down comfortably and expect the impossible to happen. It usually doesn't.

Dr. Elmer Green's brain-diagrams, limbic consciousness and chakra trip hurtled even more speedily along a scientific roller-coaster route. The thousand-petalled lotus and the inevitable Kundalini began to sound within easy and general reach as he coaxed us along with smiling confidence. It was all so simple, in spite of a statutory warning not to arouse 'that which you may not be able to handle.' It was as effective as the statutory warning issued to smokers. For there was a buzz of all-knowing responses when terms like *siddha, siddhi, bindu* and *sushumnanadi* suddenly rent the air. Neat definitions are one way of killing a concept, and mystique is a necessary veil, I concluded.

I had looked forward to the crux of the transpersonal vision—Dr. Stan Grof's and Dr. Christina Grof's combined presentation. Stan Grof outlined his experiments in psychiatry using psychedelic drug sessions and his progress to non-drug, transpersonal techniques, quite convincingly, though a shade too confidently, even arrogantly, in spite of repeated confessions of dissatisfaction. The lord did protest too much. Christina outlined her personal traumas and experience of unusual states of consciousness which she subsequently identified as possible *Kundalini* awakening. They had come to differentiate such experiences from psychoses and to treat them as spiritual emergencies. Their message—as I got it—"you have it too (the *Kundalini*). Awaken it, help it along with our transpersonal techniques. We have formed the Spiritual Emergency Network—SEN for short—which will make it all more widespread and workable. Details available at the next lecture. *Kundalini* for me, *Kundalini* for you, *Kundalini* for one and all."

I came away distinctly disturbed. Let sleeping *Kundalinis* lie, was my instinctive, and partly conditioned response. When they are ready to rise, they will do so. They certainly don't need to be jogged any more than a cart-load of dynamite or explosives. And how do you package the *Kundalini* for mass consumption? It is a very special, exclusive, strictly prescribed, carefully supervised and hard-to-follow spiritual diet. One man's meat, we all acknowledge, can be another man's poison. *Kundalini* is strong meat that is poison for most people. And cautions, for anyone who is dealing with tantric concepts, need to be very much more than statutory. They need to be emphasised. I felt apprehensive for the many hopefuls who would want the *Kundalini* roused and out in six rapid moves; and for the many more who would make a full-time non-occupation out of it in their rush for liberation.

But there were those who trod the path slowly and carefully. Frances Vaughan was among them. She delineated the Transpersonal Self (a healthy, inclusive integration of body, mind and spirit), outlined a process for summoning it, making no claims, least of all for herself. "I would like to say that I find all this easy to follow in my profession as a psychotherapist. In my personal relationships I find it more difficult to do so." After she stated the first instruction, 'Quiet the Mind', she added truthfully, 'very simple, very difficult'. I found that more persuasive than a strident, triumphal march to transpersonality.

And, of course, there was the genuine messiah who arrived to sweep me off my complacent feet for the second time in my life—Mother Teresa. She fused science and spirituality in one easy angel-leap. "There is no greater science than the science of love", she pronounced as she shone out on us. She was truly transcendental, truly a 'transperson'. She did and she prayed as she thought and she felt, frail and bent with the strength that she held and contained for all mankind. She spoke in the level, unstressed tones of total conviction, she made no overstatements, no understatements. She couldn't—and didn't need to.

I am not questioning the need for a conference of this kind. But it certainly needed to provide more time and facilities for doubts to be raised. The Kundalini can only rise from the ocean or mire of doubt; it is not for nothing that the lotus rises from a bed of slush or the goddess Shri from a churning ocean of conflict between the gods and the demons. No consensus of opinion can really emerge without a pooling of doubt struggling to see the light of day. The tone of the conference smacked overly of certainty.

Mirtala Bentov was next on my list. She was a woman, a sculptress in bronze, and between the terse lines of her listing in the Conference brochure lurked a mystic, scarcely veiled. As it turned out, I had picked a winner. It is not everyday that one meets an unashamed visionary, riddled with doubts yet certain of one thing—that the spirit prevails, that man lives not by bread alone, that the concrete is to be looked at and seen through till one confronts consciousness, the self, the spirit. And as a creative artist, she had a medium, a vocabulary which articulated clearly and strongly the adventures of her soul.

"I am really not much of an organisation person. I work alone. But it is reassuring to be part of a like-minded association where people from all over the world, in all walks of life, get together to reaffirm the spiritual needs of human beings."

A fortnight later, after a day spent conversing on art, reality and illusion, she admitted, "in the West where science and rationality have reigned supreme for so long, one can be terribly alone in one's spiritual search. You need props."

I started off with a question on how all this deliberate, determined exercising of the spirit had affected her creativity. "For one thing, it gave me an insight into my creative processes. Guided meditation helped me reconstruct the creative moment. I got to know the process—the striving, the churning emotion, the individuation and at the very last, the reality of art when thought makes contact with form. I began to understand the creative moment, the fusion of form with idea."

My next question hesitantly skirted what seemed an important issue. I had glanced through her two books, *Thought-forms* and *Mandalas*. Later I was to see her audio-visual, 'The Human Journey'. Sculpture and poetry stood side by side, unmistakably speaking the language of Eastern, particularly Indian, mysticism. What had triggered it?

Mirtala was like an excited student, reliving her graduation. "As a young art student, I was given a routine assignment. I was asked to make a replica of the Nataraja bronze at the Boston Museum. I knew almost nothing of the myth—it was a set task and I worked hard at it. By the time I had finished, I felt deeply stirred. It was as if the bronze spoke to me through centuries of worship and faith. I was totally tuned in to its vibrations. That's when, I think, my spiritual trip really began."

Mirtala's husband, a scientist and, according to her, a realized soul, reinforced and strengthened her faith. In the personal storm that followed his death in an air-crash, she nearly drowned, clutching at spiritual straws which blessedly turned into a steadying anchor.

"My work now speaks for me—both my sculpture and my poetry. Poetry is a linear progression, sculpture speaks in rounded wholeness. It takes shape in my consciousness, full-blown and near-complete. My poetry is more embryonic, unfolding in steps.

Looking back on her Nataraja experience she said, "Art is mostly transformation of external impressions, the impact of the environment on the senses; with me, particularly, the visual sense. After the Nataraja, my creative experience was internalised. I didn't depend on outside impressions any more."

Mirtala's imagery is powerful. Her bronzes never more than two or three feet, image an inward journey through a spiritual landscape signposted with visionary insights— spheres that divide to disclose, figures reaching out to each other, spires and ascents of light and shade, hollow and peak, solid masses sculpted with peepholes into the cosmic consciousness, there to feel, to know, to recognise. The tight bud of the soul, the opening lotus of the consciousness, the vaulting angel-form of the released spirit, the branching regeneration in the deadweight of concrete—all these form a definite vocabulary, fashioned assiduously to handle matters of the spirit.

"The spirit speaks, reaches out. A mother with a very sick, dying child once borrowed a sculpture of mine which she could not afford to buy. It was inspired by a dead tree-trunk, sprouting new life. Knowing nothing of this, she and the child both saw in it an affirmation of life. It helped the child's recovery. How do we explain away such things? Should we?"

Mirtala had spent two weeks in an ashram. What did it do for her? "It gave me space to grow, to be still. And the chanting of Sanskrit prayers and mantras—they move me deeply. It is not an escape. I go back to work with renewed energy. You see, my view of art is very positive. The artistic processes do not merely perceive reality. They create it."

I could not here help airing my pet perception, gleaned from grazing on Indian spiritual pastures. "Reality is only the path to Truth. Maya, or manifestation, is real but not true. It is a fact to be gone beyond. That is where the spirit comes in."

We had talked for four hours. As Mirtala packed her bags for a final week at Ganeshpuri Ashram, we said our last words, on non-attachment—I, a refugee from Burma whose father died the year after we got to India and she, a Ukrainian who had walked her way to freedom, trying to blot out memories of a father to whom Siberia had happened. "I have come to terms with material possessions. I shall never forget how, near the very end of our journey, we felt the first warmth of spring. I looked at my only piece of precious clothing, a fur coat. With absolutely no regrets I hung it up on a tree and walked on, feeling light and less burdened. As for national boundaries, they were the first to be erased. The spirit has no country."

Mirtala is a fine product of American academics, a beautiful flowering of the American mind at its seeking best. A graduate of Tufts University, she was nourished and nurtured by the intellectual activity that Boston is famous for. Listed in three Who's Whos and two international dictionaries, Mirtala is now, in the best Eastern traditions, a student of life, always learning, ever doubting. I told her as we parted that what attracted me most to her was her questioning self. Anyone so full of doubt is bound to come face-to-face with the certainty of Truth. Anyone so full of beginnings merits a happy ending.

Myth in Comic Form

The term 'comic' covers a wide literary field—too wide for it to be brushed aside as an unsatisfactory and undesirable mode of story-telling. There are fun-comics, horror-comics, comics that spin out characters larger than life who hold the common reader spell-bound with admiration, and serious comics (an apparent contradiction in terms)—comics that retell classics, folk tales, forgotten myth and difficult history. This last, the comic that retells, stands uneasily apart, on the outer fringes of acceptance. Adults look upon it with suspicion, children find it bland, lacking in 'sensational' appeal. Yet it is making slow, but steady inroads wherever necessary into the area of formal reading matter.

Comics in general or cartoons, are a genre which is disliked, and despised by the guardians of right reading; liked, acclaimed and devoured by young readers. The adult reaction is established and the arguments familiar. The language tends to slang, the matter is light and packaged for too easy and casual a reading, demanding no concentration or mental application whatsoever. This is what the comic strip can, and very often does, become. But we cannot overlook its tremendous power for good and its great strength, its acceptability amongst an age-group which is vulnerable and open to influences. If we can swallow our distaste for comics—and thinking of Dennis the Menace, Asterix, Peanuts and Tin Tin will help—it is a medium we can ill afford to ignore. In this striking, proven, established and totally accepted medium of speaking pictures acting out a story, we have the right sugar-coating—and there is no better way of administering a pill.

This leads me to a specific area—the conversion of ancient literary material into contemporary reading matter, making use of the form, merely, of the comic strip or cartoon. In this highly underrated form is contained an instrument of propagation that is hard to beat. In its disjointed continuity lies a flexibility that very few print media have. Frame by frame, it can tell a continuous story. And yet, because it proceeds in separate units, it allows for a kind of variation that more leisurely, flowing forms like the short story do not permit. Changes of mood, situation, leaps over time and space, can be made simply and credibly.

One may well ask why this laborious—for it is laborious—process, this somewhat parasitical activity, this battening on old forgotten tales, this chewing the cud of tradition?

The collective myth, history, legend, folklore and literature of a people constitute a precious commodity.

The past is part of the present and should be taken forward into the future. This process of the past being absorbed into the present, assimilated and taken forward into the future is normally automatic. In the case of India, recent history has interrupted, and, to some extent, arrested, this perfectly natural process. Two hundred years of British domination have given us a language and set of values that are not just alien but deceptively adequate. The myth and legend of India, particularly in the urban educated are no longer alive or active—images of the past neither excite nor trouble us. Our children grow up in a sort of cultural vacuum which Western pop music and western myth just cannot fill. It is vital that they know who Sita was, if only to comprehend their mothers and their maids. It is important that they know all about Bhima, for only then will they understand the champion wrestlers and the strong men of the films. It is good for them to learn about Vikramaditya, the fabled king, who spent a whole night tramping up and down a gruesome cemetery while a ghostly spirit quizzed him on life and in the process, slowly, but surely, drove home the point that his wisdom was challengeable. With the twenty-fifth story-riddle, Vikramaditya finally failed a test, was stumped for an answer. Simultaneously as dawn flushed the sky, wisdom dawned on the King in an inimitable and typically Oriental manner—the truth that he did not know all, came to him.

A profoundly philosophical idea, almost too deep for communication. And yet, the truth has been taught to a king—or to a child, for royalty in its flush of pride and power is child-like. Twenty-five enchanting stories, crisp and spell-binding, are held in a frame-work which in itself is a master story-telling gimmick—a world-renowned king, spending the night with a ghoulish spirit, a *vetala,* who rides his back. The book has everything—suspense, humour, action and immense story value. Why lose it? And why pass up the opportunity to administer your child a dose of authentic Indian magic?

How does one recast ancient literature? How does one handle the hallowed and the sacrosanct which has in addition, gathered to itself the awesome mystery of the unfamiliar? How does one cope with a glorious past and its profundity? How does one, in short, blow the gold-dust off a halo?

There are problems, particularly if one chooses the comic format. It is a mode of narrative that has gathered about it anything but respectable associations. To get the parent's or the teacher's seal of approval, to make them see it stripped of its unholy accretions, is a hurdle that the writer of comics has to face. This can be tackled only by consistently high standards of language, illustration and choice of subject matter. The day will come when the 'serious' comic will have carved itself out a niche, when it will cease to be furtively read by disapproving adults or allowed to stand on library shelves merely on sufferance.

A classic has a distinct character of its own. To adapt it is a challenge to inventiveness, if not to high creativity. Take the *Mahabharata,* for instance. Story leads to story, at every point, going backwards, forwards, sideways and in circles. It is like a spherical, three-dimensional labyrinth which leads somewhere definitely but takes an infinity of verses to do so. The tangles have a meaning, a method. To retell it for children is a gigantic task. First, to separate the strands. Second, to select and reject, and to never lose sight of the total meaning of the great work or damage its pattern.

Some ancient works need building upon. They are terse, pithy outlines which need filling out to read well and maintain the child's interest. The Vikramaditya stories are a good case in point. Here is ideal material for retelling; to sift, rebalance, modify and retell without distortion is a pleasurable task.

And then the language. To put words into the mouth of characters frozen into attitudes many centuries old and having the lineaments of fading frescoes—this is the most challenging task of all. The language must not be so obviously 'current' as to destroy the 'period' flavour. Yet, one must avoid the most common pitfall—precious quaintness. And all this, while reeling under the impact of either the sombre original or the equally stately English translations. It is climbing uphill all the way. The speech 'balloons' are ridiculous when peppered too generously with 'Reverend Sire', 'O holy one' and 'Thy humble servant awaits thy pleasure'. On the other hand modernity can jar. Take a Jataka tale. These are parables of the Buddha centred round the *Bodhisattvas*—previous incarnations of the Buddha. One cannot make a Bodhisattva, even if he's a monkey, say things like

'Breakfast, here I come'. One cannot show him, even if he's only a deer in a twentieth-century comic strip, marching off, tankard in hand, looking for a forest pool and thinking aloud 'I must have a drink'. Yet such absurdities exist in retold comics. To strike the right balance, sound the right note, is all-important. Old tales must be true to their own times, while speaking effectively to children of today. That is the only valid yardstick to apply. If they are presented wrong, they risk outright rejection, or worse, invite ridicule.

What about the relentless uniformity of a fixed length of, usually, thirty-two pages? It caters, for one thing, to the normal attention-span of a child or, for that matter, of a busy adult. For another, it imposes a discipline on the writer. The framework is a fillip to inventiveness and ingenuity, rather than a clamp. The hard work and sweat that goes into a story-strip leads to a designed, desired result. There is little scope for deviations into vapid description or comment—a vice that retellers of old tales are very often guilty of. Any dawdling is strictly ruled out.

How much gets left out? Much. But then, a retold story is never meant to be an end in itself. It sows the seed of an interest that might one day flower into a genuine curiosity about the original. If the retelling leaves a memory that can awaken into a later adult interest, it has done enough. Our problem is to substitute the widespread, oral retelling with the written, illustrated comic strip, to speak to a generation that might otherwise never know of the existence of these great works, to catch them young, to take these stories out of inaccessible old volumes and return them to the mainstream of life where they belong.

We have a body of literature which is almost untouchable in its remote splendour. We need to access this material and see that it gets through to a generation sadly in need of establishing contact with its own receding past. We have had the very good idea of doing this through the most powerful existing narrative medium—the comic strip or the story strip.

The fact that the form is incompatible with the contents should not deter us; for without this short and easy cut, the way to the classics is an obstacle race the child never even begins to run. The comic strip seems to offer the most effective way of achieving the impossible.

Music as Worship

The best of India was on display as Great Britain celebrated the Festival of India. In March 1982, when it began, a Shakespearean spring was in the air. 'Violets that come before the swallow dares. And take the winds of March with beauty', and, we were told, it made way gracefully for a fleeting passage of Indian-summer warmth.

The expectant Londoner was being exposed to what is true and abiding, as well as current, in Indian culture as it went flooding into galleries, shops, theatres and music halls. The Anglo-India of curry, colonels and memsahibs wilting in fanblown heat, of nabobs, nostalgia and palace pleasures is common knowledge. But the mainstream of Indian cultural traditions was bound to come as somewhat of a surprise.

Among those taking the music of India to London was Ustad Aminuddin Dagar. He was the upholder of a musical tradition that has survived against great odds. For the school of Dhrupad singing adapts uneasily and reluctantly to modern concert conditions. It clings tenaciously to its temple origins. The musical delineation is devotional throughout, aiming to lift both singer and audience into the realms of the spirit. Today, when the sublime is all too often the ridiculous, such a stance can lead to awkwardness. This is the basic Dhrupad hurdle. And Aminuddin Dagar crossed it everytime. For he was to the Dhrupad manner born, and highly bred.

I was half-prepared for a plunge into the deep waters of the spirit when I went to meet him, through years of exposure to his music. He was unquestionably singer and saint-in-the-making.

"Dhrupad is Dhruvapad, the path of steadfastness", he declared as he went on to equate the *alap*, the musical introduction, to the aarti, the ritual worship with lighted lamps. "You invoke a *raga* as surely as you invoke a deity. As a raga progresses, the form, the sleeping deity, comes awake and takes musical shape. It is there for you to see, to feel, to experience. That is the purpose of music".

Here I must relate a strange incident. Sitting in an old church turned into a studio in a Swedish coastal town, my artist friend suddenly said, "I must play you some music I bought blindly when I was in India. I had no time to ask around. I just walked into a record shop, asked for a few records to be played and picked these". I waited for Ravi Shankar or Ali Akbar to come on. But the notes that rose to fill the arched and domed interior of this alien house of God were from a record by the Dagar brothers. There was no mistaking the devotional mood either. It had reached across all man-made barriers. Her other choice was a record of Subbulakshmi's.

The hard work that goes into all religious and mystic experience goes into Dhrupad. Practice makes perfect, practice that never lets up. Aminuddin cited the family maxim on regular practice: "One day's practice given up puts an artist back by a hundred days".

Voice training is a mantric exercise and Aminuddin Dagar related it to *pranayama* in yoga. Both have to do with life-breath and hidden sources of the self. Ustad Aminuddin or Banne Bhaiyya, as he was affectionately called, next demonstrated the various sound-effects that voice-training aimed at—the snake's sway, the tremor, the swing, the leaping over notes and back, the peal of temple bells, the chest note and many others. All this, so to say, was a daily clearing of the throat, so that music at its divine best could flow through a seasoned channel.

I asked about words in music. "The true musical mantra is the transmutation of words into pure sound. Our alap does that. Embedded in the alap is a definite string of words. In the elaboration they are transformed into sounds which lead into the mood, the experience."

In the age of amorality, Banne Bhaiyya's morality stood out with monolithic strength. "Truth, *satya* is essential for a musician. Otherwise he cannot strike a true note". And truth, for Aminuddin Dagar, stemmed from devotion, faith, religion.

"A musician should be so devotional that unbelievers listening to him should turn into believers." His vocabulary was wholly spiritual and religious. "The daily musical offering should be the *surya namaskar* (oblations to the rising sun)".

Banne Bhaiyya spoke quite comfortably and spontaneously about his chosen celibate way of life.

"The true artist is a complete person, knowing and experiencing everything. The experience of love can be equally fulfilling and complete when it is directed towards a brother and guru, as mine was".

What he said next put him for me into a special class of seers.

"The bliss of enjoyment (*bhog*) can never be as ecstatic as the bliss of sacrifice (*tyag*)". Of all the things that he had said, that struck the truest and most traditional note. And it was the most eloquent statement I had come across on *sannyasa*, the last and most difficult of all the *ashrama dharmas*, the four stages of a true Hindu's journey through life.

Music for the Gods

The Kaveri flows down the centuries in a wealth of fable and legend. In the district of Tanjavur it spreads wide and beautiful round the island village of Tiruvaiyaru where it joins four other rivers. Here, in the middle of the 18th century, it flowed sweet music during the life-time of Thyagaraja, saint musician and devotee of Rama.

Local tradition has it that the Kaveri waters hone the dull brain to razor sharpness, touch mortal clay and turn it to the gold of creativity. Hence Ramanuja's mathematical feats—and Thyagaraja, who sang to Rama, his chosen deity, in 24,000 songs composed in 211 *ragas*, forming the inspired bulk of classical Carnatic music.

Thyagaraja's music defies glib classification. It is tradition-bound and restricted. But like all great art, it bursts its bounds repeatedly. The form becomes a mere vehicle pouring out in endless melody the glories of Rama, turning the *bhava* or experience of *bhakti* into the *rasa* or aesthetic flavour of music.

The Indian bhakti tradition gives the mystic experience a quality of immediacy, dragging it down from the colourless heights of abstract spirituality into the familiar realms of human experience. The convention of *ishtadevata* whereby you choose your own god, makes worship an intensely personal affair. No guilt accompanies this act of survey, selection and rejection. It is considered as natural as the choice of a life partner and as necessary. Through the arduous journey of living, one needs a divine court of appeal. In the hands of a bhakta or devotee, through the intimate handling of a life-time—of fondling, coaxing, pleading, haranguing, accusing, loving, adoring, taunting, scolding, by in fact, running the gamut of human emotions—the *ishtadevata* ends up being a creature of the devotee's making. It emerges bathed in the colours of the bhakta's experience and in the fashioning of this deity lies the *mukti* or salvation of the bhakta.

Every life-time is marked by a search for the ideal relationship. As long as it is confined to earthly ties, perfection eludes, and the search is endless. For the bhakta it ends when he finds his deity and loses himself—and throughout his life the end is clearly in sight. When the bhakta happens to be a musician, the wonder of union with god and the truth of salvation is brought within general reach.

Thyagaraja is heady stuff. Listening to his music, one is rewarded with fleeting glimpses of an intensely experienced relationship with god. The futile controversies that seek to separate matter from spirit, tangible from intangible, earth from heaven, man from god dissolve, and *terra firma* slips from under one's leaden feet. For those of us who 'lay waste our powers getting and spending', this could be the beginning of an adventure into the realms of ecstasy, the mystic's natural element.

Driving past verdant fields and groves and limpid streams in the magic month of *margazhi,* month of harvest and plenty, the spectacle of nature was disturbing enough to crack the crust and soften the callus of big city living. But Thyagaraja was no unschooled rustic wandering the gold-green fields of Tiruvaiyaru, struck by the marvels of nature into inspired lunacy. His discovery of the spirit had more erudite beginnings. His grandfather was Giri Raja Brahman of Tiruvarur, scholar and musician of note, favoured at court and honoured by the king. His father, Rama Brahman was a Shiva bhakta who fell in love with Tiruvaiyaru while on a visit there and chose to move there with his wife and family of three sons. To the youngest and most gifted, Thyagaraja, named after the Lord of Tiruvarur, Shiva, he passed on his practice of bhakti which in Tiruvarur became Rama bhakti. Thyagaraja went to a Sanskrit school and there, in Valmiki's *Ramayana,* he discovered the lineaments of Raghu Rama, Vishnu incarnate as king and ruler. There was no holding back. Rama occupied his being to the exclusion of all else. The music in him had found a fitting outlet and he turned it to the only use a mystic has for anything—communion with god.

Thyagaraja's music is the journal of a mystic, the story of his life with Rama. There was no situation, no time or year or season when his presence was not either strongly felt or keenly missed. As a student, as a householder, as a budding ascetic on the way to full *sannyasa*, through the four stages prescribed for the span of a Hindu's life on earth, his *ashrama dharma*, Thyagaraja clung to one vision—the vision of Rama. It was glorious one moment, clouded the very next. It took on all shapes, assumed all forms—child, parent, companion, lover, guide, preceptor. It was a blazing light that sometimes flickered, often failed as he stumbled blindly through the dark forests of the spirit.

The Thyagaraja Festival of Music at Tiruvaiyaru must be seen in this context. It is termed an *aradhana* or offering, an annual ritual that substitutes for the *shraddha* or annual death ceremony of the normal householder, for saints do not die, they attain *samadhi*, they are *muktas*, liberated from the vicious cycle of life and death.

It began as a spontaneous sanctification ritual. Musicians came from all over, sat near the *samadhi* and sang. Some years ago, Bangalore Nagaratnamma, a well-known musician, came to Tiruvaiyaru, built a temple on the spot where Thyagaraja had attained *samadhi*, thus making it a focal point of music and *bhakti*. The annual gathering gradually grew into a body of like-minded music enthusiasts and in the early years of this century it began to take formal shape as an organised festival of Carnatic music. On *Bahula panchami,* in the month of *margazhi* in the year 1847, Thyagaraja attained *samadhi*. This day is the high point of the festival.

As I walked up to the immense canopied area strewn with clean, dry sand, flanked by the Kaveri, past eating shops and peanut vendors, I wondered whether the festival would turn into a noisy jamboree. The printed programme did little to quiet my fears. More than eighty musicians, some allotted as short a period as five minutes, were to perform. I settled down apprehensively for the ribbon-cutting, speeches by the collector, local politician, veteran singer and the musical story-teller, the Harikatha exponent.

From the very start it was apparent that this was no ordinary concert. The star was Thyagaraja, the presiding deity, Rama, the congregation whoever they were, wherever they had come from and whatever they were going back to, a congregation of *bhaktas* poised for a brief but very real entry into the charmed circle of a mystic experience.

The nasal, drawn-out notes of the *nadaswaram* ushered in the festival and its opening artist, Yesudasan, play-back singer from India's Bollywood, a contemporary legend of youth bitten by the spiritual bug, a Christian whose inspiration is Lord Ayyappan of Shabari. A man for all gods, fearlessly and, I realized, most humbly treading the razor's edge of the *Upanishads*, the path to salvation.

Part of one's experience of Thyagaraja is a visit to his house. I entered the dwelling of a man who had possessed nothing, my head humming with the past. And then came my windfall, my spiritual scoop.

Yesudasan entered with renowned violinist Krishnan and one or two others to pay homage to Thyagaraja. We moved to leave as it seemed an intrusion into a very private world but as Krishnan spontaneously turned to someone next to him and asked for his 'fiddle' and suggested to Yesudasan that they 'perform', the manager gestured to us to stay. We were glued to the cold, hard floor listening with bated breath to the impromptu offering. It is not everyday that die-hard city dwellers are treated to a close-up brush with the spirit or witness the mechanics of mysticism.

On the third and last day of the festival, Thyagaraja's *samadhi* was celebrated in a ritual that enacted his life. Musicians assembled at his house, sang in prayer, walked in procession down the streets he had walked as a mendicant, receiving alms and entered the enclosure for the grand finale—a chorus of great voices singing the *Pancharatna kritis,* five compositions in ragas marked with grandeur and simplicity, with no distracting frills or embellishments.

Every year at Tiruvaiyaru, at the Aradhana festival, musicians sing Thyagaraja's *kritis* with over 6,000 people listening in prayerful concentration. Rama lives again as his name is taken, one knows, not in vain. And the Kaveri, floodlit by the moon, speaks of a saint who cast a spell on her rippling waters with the sweetness that filled his life. A fitting commemoration that keeps the memory of God alive in the hearts of listeners, for nothing so easily slips the mind of man as the thought of God.

Dance in Khajuraho

In the central heartland of India, in the middle years of time as history reckons it, between the tenth and eleventh centuries A.D. the temples of Khajuraho came to be sculpted by history and lit by legend. It was originally a complex of eighty-five temples of which only twenty-two survive. They bear the unmistakable impress of temporal power—the power of the Chandela dynasty, and the flower of its royal manhood, Chandra Varman. Such statements of power were also acknowledgements of divine grace, acts of thanksgiving which pointed to divinity as the source of all power on earth and therefore to be commemorated.

Dynasties rose, survived and maintained themselves through the grace of the powers that be, the gods. And then, as the subjects, the *praja*, in their simple faith, worshipped and sought blessings, appeased and mollified, their collective goodwill spread a canopy of divine protection over the head of the one who ruled, the *raja*.

A declaration of power through conquest, of faith in God, an expression of monumental glory—such is Khajuraho. Legend follows and blurs the facts of history. Khajuraho, some say, is named after a grove of *khajur* trees (date palms). Tradition also offers you a more dramatic legend. One magic moonlit night, the beautiful Hemavati came to bathe in the waters of a lake nearby. The moon, entranced, gazed upon her, lighting her up with his love. As their hearts caught fire, they embraced and came together. Hemavati, terrified of the consequences, bewailed her lot. But the moon God, Chandrama, soothed her. 'Of this union will be born a son who will build a fort, possess the philosopher's stone and perform a sacrifice that will wipe out all sin from this act of passion.' So, the legend says, Chandra Varman, king and builder of forts and the temples of Khajuraho, was born.

The particular glory of Khajuraho is its celebration of life as love and coupling, its explicit erotica expressing the principle of *shakti,* the energy which, coursing through the primal substance of life, breaks out as the marvels of creation, the manifold world of names and forms, the *namarupa samsara,* a world fuelling the five senses and raising the sap of life in each living creature.

Khajuraho carries this message of heightened sense perceptions leading one to liberation, the *tantric* path to salvation. *Tantra* is a dramatic alchemy of sense and sensibility, resulting in contemplation of the Infinite. Ecstasy is the way of *Tantra* and it utilises man's most available resource, sexual energy, to generate it.

Khajuraho is a celebration of life at its passionate best—its strength, its power, its sheer force.

It is to feelings and traditions such as these that we must relate the ancient rite of temple dancing as it must have been performed in Khajuraho. Each performance was a heightening of the mood of worship and prayer, invoking the deity and arousing it till its *shakti*, its power spreads over dancer and viewer alike, carrying them on waves of joy to a perception of the Infinite. And it is this powerful undercurrent of ecstatic contemplation that gives the week-long Khajuraho festival of dance a special dimension. The festival was started in the mid-eighties and is the annual highlight of the Khajuraho season.

Although the venue has shifted from the immediate vicinity of the temples, their presence now forming only a dim silhouette of a reminder, a skyline barely discernible, the dancers carry within themselves the weighty presence of a divine witness. This again is the Indian gift for internalisation with little fuss. All that is without is really held within, in the spaces of the human heart.

Yet all was not solemn and sacrosanct. Life provided a touch of the ridiculous. After all, the dance was no longer within the temple but outside it! As I sat, trying to bring into focus the temple silhouette, then the backdrop of the tree and the lush, ragged green hedge, my eyes shifted to a group of rocks, an uneasy, confused arrangement, semi-Japanese, quasi-Himalayan. In what could have been a moment of god-given humour and coincidence, a pie-dog, tail curled in mongrel nonchalance, trotted across. No one moved to chase it away, as the dancers, equally unfazed, continued to depict myth after divine myth, legend after riveting legend. The dog too went about its canine business, raised its leg against the rock, said its canine say, in a manner of speaking, and the show went on regardless, undaunted!

It was a performance of Manipuri dances. I had earlier met the dancers, watched them rehearse. Singhajit Singh said of this North-Eastern style, "It is not entertainment, it is part of our daily lives, tied up with ritual and celebration—birth, marriage, death, seasonal festivities. We still preside over these occasions and they are not stage performances".

The dancers set about creating a world of myth and legend. Krishna as a baby was crawling up to Radha's cradle as the mothers discuss a worrying condition—Radha had simply not opened her eyes since the day she was born. Suddenly joy breaks over them like a tidal wave when, the moment the child Krishna leaned over her, Radha opened her eyes to gaze upon the only face that would haunt her life-long. The sleeping beauty had awakened to the presence of her Prince Charming, the seeking soul had set eyes upon its goal. The evening ended on a highly spiritual note as Charu and Singhajit, in swaying, soft waves of movement and melody, like the heave and swell of water, lulled the audience into a mood of submergence, submergence with the Ultimate, the common destiny and destination of all striving humanity, just as the mighty Ganga is of all rivers that flow into her.

The mood stayed with me as I rode an open cycle rickshaw back to my hotel. It was only when the glare of the well-lit lobby hit my eyes, that I felt a twinge of fear in retrospect at the thought of having ridden a desolate road, in a strange town in dacoit country at dead of night. Such is the power of an inspired performance.

Abhinaya–Expressional Skills in Dance

Kalanidhi Narayanan is a Bharatanatyam dancer from Chennai who stopped short in her dancing tracks for nearly thirty years. When I met her in the early fifties, her passion for dance was no more than a deeply hidden dream in her large expressive eyes. A stray remark would betray her pre-occupation with what was obviously more than a youthful pastime. "I keep hoping I will have a daughter whom I can teach to dance", she said seriously one day, after the second of her three sons was born! When she suddenly and surprisingly resumed in the early 1970s, she instinctively turned to the one aspect of Bharatanatyam that had always fascinated her— *abhinaya*, the art of expression. What gave her strength to continue was her mentor Y.G. Doraiswamy's confidence that she had many years of fruitful teaching, if not full-scale performance, before her, and her own conviction that the rich and precious art of *abhinaya* needed to be taught as a speciality. Her pupils, students of many gurus, came to her only to deepen their knowledge and practice of *abhinaya*. Most teachers, quite rightly, treat *abhinaya* as just a part of the whole exercise of dance, and most students fail to see the vast potential of this aspect of dance.

"It is an endless process, *abhinaya*—I never stop learning. Even while teaching, in the middle of a phrase, I see new meanings."

There are only two challenges that *abhinaya* faces— one's capacity to train every muscle, every glance every movement of the eyebrow, every turn of the face and body and through these to portray what passes through one's heart. In the best *abhinaya* it is difficult to decide which plays the more important part—the capacity to feel or the capacity to express.

Watching Kalanidhi teach is a very special treat. It is a modification of the old *gurukul* system—the teacher is revered, but not unquestioningly and unconditionally.

Demonstrating a *nayika* at her toilette, she would say in her very gentle, firm and coaxing tones—"There are many ways of dressing up. Think of yourself. There is one mood and manner for dressing to meet your friends, another to greet your husband, yet another for your lover—and of course, for dressing to go to the office." Sitting cross-legged, with only a supporting hand gesture, she would project the precise emotion—the flutter of a young heart as it draped a silken garment, gazed into a flattering mirror, patted a flower into place on coiled, scented tresses, outlined an eye with *kohl* in preparation for an evening of side-long glances and burgeoning love. Gradually, through the sessions, the pupil's face would mirror the emotion as it filtered through her own consciousness, not merely duplicate it. One could sense an *absorption,* not a copy of a style.

Kalanidhi has gathered round her a dedicated band of students and connoisseurs. Her performances are simple, undramatic events linked to small audiences with a taste for the rare, the unusual, the forgotten. Hers is a programme for unearthing, resuscitation and constant creation, to unveil the mysteries of facial expression and body language in dance; to go beyond the dictionary of gestures into worlds of buried meaning, to read between the *mudras,* over and above the facial gymnastics that *abhinaya* reduced to its rudimentary function, very often tends to be.

Although intensely spiritual, almost mystic, in her approach to dance, she believes firmly in the validity of depicting human frailties in the emotional sphere. What comes across in Kalanidhi's carefully selected repertoire of *padams* (songs and poems) is the human situation— its dignity, its ludicrousness, its grandeur, its pathos, its helplessness, its humour. Imperceptibly and unobtrusively, Kalanidhi trains her audience to look for the shade, the nuance, the undercurrents in Bharatanatyam which has so much spectacle to offer visually that it can easily distract the unschooled eye.

One is familiar with feats of unbridled creativity, of larger-than-life achievements. It is rarer to see what wonders the creative spirit, when checked and even curbed, can attain. The beauty of Kalanidhi's work is the beauty of the contained, disciplined, inward-delving mind enriched with the stuff that all great art is made of— the stuff of experience.

"Perhaps the break in my dancing career has matured me. The depths of meaning I see in a *padam* now may not have been possible earlier. I notice this in my students too. I know they are beginning to grow when they slow down, are less easily satisfied, more reluctant to 'finish' a *padam*".

Research, restoration, reconstruction and resuscitation call for a very special kind of creative effort especially in the field of the performing arts. All these activities have to do with recreating and communicating traditions that are in constant danger of dying out; vanishing like ghosts at dawn into thin air. In a country like ours, blessed with an all-inclusive, common, binding cultural life-force and burdened with divisive, localised, at times separatist, multi-lingual traditions, the task of breathing life into dying cultural forms and images becomes a complex and somewhat daunting task.

The resurgence of the national spirit during and after Independence brought with it a sustained, frenzied and self-conscious revival of Indian arts, crafts, textiles, dance, music and even ritual—in fact, the whole Indian way of life which had fallen into disuse, especially in town and city. It was as if a proud and patient lion had wisely decided to slumber through bad days till the time came for flexing his golden body and striding out into the sun once again. It was a joyous awakening but also somewhat self-conscious, self-absorbed and very often occupied with externals, with the mere trappings of being Indian. It was a narcissistic, uncritical, at times undiscerning fascination with the pageantry of India—its colours, its patterns, its sounds.

In a dance form like Bharatanatyam, there is much, almost too much, that appeals to the senses—the costumes, the face, the figure, the mime, the rhythm, the music—the whole spectacle of colour, light and sound through which, like a dazzling jewel, the dancer, almost always a woman, expresses the eternal verities of the human emotions. It can be distractingly pretty, lull the audience into a passive cultural stupor of contentment and deaden their response to the essence of any performance—the masterly depiction of feeling through mood. Indeed as any connoisseur will testify, the unwary viewer can come away from a performance which entertains without stirring into life the rasika, the enjoyer, the responder lying dormant in each one of us and the rousing of which is the real justification of any performing art.

Kalanidhi's achievement lies in subordinating the more distracting aspects of even abhinaya, expression, to a serious depiction of the essential emotion of a lyric. The predominant flavour of her performances is the emotion of love, the shringara rasa. She feels that this emotion encompasses almost the entire gamut of human experience and allows for nuances and complexities that the other rasas do not have scope for. She is not too far from the truth—love is, after all, a many-splendoured thing. Even *bhakti*, devotion, takes on colour only when the object of devotion is approached with the madness of love.

In her search for dance lyrics that aptly express love through *abhinaya*, Kalanidhi has tapped many literary and musical sources, prime among them being the saint-composers Kshetrayya, Annamacharya, Jayadeva and the Alwars of the Vaishnavite tradition. Through the exploration of mainly the Krishna legend as sung and chanted by these madmen of God, Kalanidhi has built up a repertoire which depicts the experience of love as the Indian has understood and experienced it. The love of mother for child, man for woman, saint for God, the human situations that give rise to and result from this sweet affliction called love—the injured wife, the triumphant mistress, the married woman helplessly and hopelessly in love with the divine charmer, Krishna, the professional courtesan conducting her inherited trade with dignity and consummate skill. There are no value judgments, no moral condemnations or praise for the rigid, accepted social prototypes. The hurt wife, instead of weeping and wailing, can be tolerant, forgiving and confident in the return of a man with whom she has spent an ecstatic youth; the strutting mistress is forgiven her short-lived triumph as the wife lays the blame for her behaviour at the door of her slavishly doting husband. The courtesan is depicted as showing great good sense when she admonishes her weak companion and instructs her to shut the door in the face of any man, be he Shiva, Vishnu, Ganesha, Subrahmanya or Krishna himself, if he comes to their house empty-handed. The realism of this piece is astoundingly modern. Good business management and professionalism is clearly not a new thing.

The many pranks of Krishna are a rich resource for *abhinaya*. A *gopi* fondling what she thinks is a child is confronted by a Krishna who kisses her full and passionately on the lips like a grown man. There is no end to the love games of Krishna or to interpretations that even today, a dancer with imagination and the subtle weapons of *abhinaya* can make, taking off from a given lyric. Reading between the lines, constructing a mood, choosing the right expressions of face, hands, body and dress, a skilled and devoted dancer can invest our ancient traditions with the flesh, blood and breath of a living, pulsating culture. In a country where any verbal or written communication is faced with more than a dozen linguistic stumbling blocks, the universal language of dance, *abhinaya,* through a training of interested audiences, can perform the task of cultural transmission effectively and enjoyably. Kalanidhi, through carefully programmed and choreographed concerts and aptly framed English explanations, has achieved precisely this. She acquaints her audience with the best that was written, sung, chanted and danced through the artistry of *abhinaya* of which beyond doubt she is among the very best exponents this country can boast of. And she has trained a generation of dancers who are following in her footsteps, keeping time with their feet to the beat of her inspired, spiritual rhythms.

The Ramayana as Ballet

Like a sixth sense or a fourth dimension there is an added man-made season, particularly in metro towns—a season for culture heralded by whatever nip the local air is capable of.

The Delhi art season has a self-conscious sense of its role as projector of Indian culture to a watching, assessing world audience of diplomats and tourists. Mumbai is almost blasé in its acceptance of the culture of India which it welcomes with easy grace. Kolkata has limited fare aimed at audiences which are not too adventurous in their culture-safaris. Chennai gathers all its talents, mainly local, as *sabhas* big and small welcome dancing feet, twanging instruments, throbbing drums and sounds that once filled temple halls and courtyards. The fine line dividing entertainment from devotion is still miraculously there. And the uniqueness of the Chennai experience is the thrill the audience experiences when artiste after artiste, according to their capacity, goes over the edge, surprising us with their moments of welcome madness.

The high, dramatic points of the Chennai season, the main attention-getters, are the Music Academy and Kalakshetra—two bastions of the South Indian performing arts that swing into action in December and January. The dance form in Kalakshetra ballets is mainly Bharatanatyam in its classical, pristine, serious temple style with no innovative concessions to lightness. Kathakali is used for its drama elements—humour, supernatural episodes and masculine, virile representations of super-men, heroes and gods. The content is historical and has epic sources.

Kalakshetra has a genesis that has shaped and moulded its style—austere, disciplined, elevated. In the beginning was the message, so to say, and it was spiritual—shorn of all elements, deliberately, that would sully its strong, fine odour of sanctity. The creative fires of Kalakshetra raise distinctly holy smoke. Rukmini Devi's ballet-blooms, indeed, her whole garden of culture, are pruned and shaped to hothouse perfection with painstakingly beautiful design. There is no room for creative happenstance or accident except within a carefully crafted and highly-structured pattern. Which is also why there are no individual flights, only inspired group activity and teamwork master-minded by a woman whose spiritual and aesthetic reach leaves one consistently dazzled.

S. Sharada, a close associate of Rukmini Devi, and prime researcher in the composition of Kalakshetra ballets reminisced, "you must remember that Kalakshetra was started at a time when temple dancing had been publicly denounced by giants like C.P. Ramaswamy Iyer and Srinivasa Shastry. For a young and beautiful woman, a Theosophist, to dance herself and to champion the cause of a decadent and socially decried art was an act of great courage."

It was a long and difficult haul—their first fumbling attempts to produce a traditional *Kuravanji* dance drama, to prise closely guarded secrets and transplant temple traditions, their bouts with reluctant maestros who were adept in the fine art of non-cooperation. "Would you believe it, it was only when our first pair of cymbals were delivered to us that we realized one was iron and the other bell-metal—that's how jealously the *nattuvanars* guarded their trade secrets."

"We were truly blessed in our musicians though. Giants composed for us, gave freely of their gift and transformed everything we presented into rivers of great music, music composed specially for dance." Tiger Varadachariar, Mysore Vasudevachar and Papanasam Sivan are big names in music. Kalakshetra's latter-day giant was M.D. Ramanathan, whose performance at the festival was one of the most memorable I have ever experienced. To a regrettably small audience, the great man gave of his anguish, perhaps, at the heedlessness of the general public in the face of genius.

Going back to the dances, what impressed me anew was the ability of a Kalakshetra ballet, classical, traditional, heavy as it is, to keep a modern audience tied to its seat. A Kalakshetra performance is a multi-level, aesthetic experience providing almost total satisfaction to our craving for beauty. Impeccable costuming enhances the human form with no hint of exhibitionism. This is a major Kalakshetra triumph. Rarely in dance does one see such unmistakable celebration of femininity in manner, in movement, in glance, in costume. And Kalakshetra does all this without the aid of bared midriff and contours straining against garments calculated to titillate. Swirls of fabric softly draped over curving hip and sloping shoulder or bunched and falling in swinging cascades of colour are all a designer's dream. Sex comes refined and triple-distilled to be savoured as a gift of the gods to man's higher instincts, not his bestial cravings.

Sharada commented on Rukmini Devi's sense of colour. "How often it has happened that long after she has chosen and allotted colours we discover in some ancient text the prescribed colours for those roles—she has arrived at them intuitively."

Kalakshetra's major achievement is the ardour and arduousness that belong to all expeditions of the human spirit; creativity here is controlled, moulded and directed down the straight and narrow path of a chosen goal— the rescue of an ancient and highly developed art from its mire of decadence, even depravity. The dance, banished from the temple, very nearly went out of all our lives. Many individuals have done pioneering work in restoring dignity and high seriousness to Bharatanatyam. But the influence and impact of Kalakshetra and Rukmini Devi have bred a generation of dancers, flawless in taste and spiritual in approach. To study and live and grow up in the environs of Kalakshetra is to be exposed to the magic of the ancient Indian dream—a fusion of all that's beautiful in the world of the senses offered up to the high reaches of man's spirit. At a Kalakshetra performance, one's feet are firmly planted on earth while the mind wanders the mazes of devotion.

At the 1982 festival, every evening feted a guest of honour—the Maharani of Travancore, noted scholars and musicians. On the last day, before the curtain went up on the concluding *Ramayana* sequence, Rukmini Devi spoke, revealing clearly her sights for Kalakshetra. "Today there will be no special guest. You are all special guests. If there is a special guest it is Rama, whose presence, I hope, you will all clearly feel before the drama ends."

The festival ended with a flourish of ritual chanting. The dramatic illusion was almost complete and the stage turned into a temple hall. It was as if, by an effort of will, the temple had been made to come to the dancer since she could no longer go to the temple. In most of us, I am sure, a responsive chord was struck, a spring touched off. In me, certainly, a fountain of inner light played, transforming the 'dreary desert sand of dead habit' into a garden of flame.

Spirit of Music

India's greatest resource is a spiritual heritage with a
formidable and unbroken lineage. Her mineral wealth,
her famed coffers of gold and gems have been plundered
and depleted over the centuries. Beset by poverty,
weakened by greed, ravaged by corruption and lack of
good governance, the country still holds together because
of it. There are moments, and those are many, when every
Indian stands with eyes lowered and head bowed in
embarrassment, even shame. But for those who care to
quarry, her spiritual mines still yield veins of pure gold.
It is our unique and inexhaustible resource.

It was in the summer of 1974, while in England, that
my third eye, so to speak, opened wide to let this truth
in, voiced by that mother of mothers, Mother Teresa, in her
famous interview with Malcolm Muggeridge. It was the
year Satyajit Ray arrived in London to open the London
Film Festival with the film 'Seema Baddha'—a first for
Indian cinema, if memory serves me right. I was reminded
afresh of what had put him and Indian cinema on the

map—the bittersweet song of Indian poverty sung on celluloid by *Pather Panchali*, his first film. It was drenched with the *bhava*, the emotion, of compassion, but what it evoked was the *rasa*, the flavour, of pity. And what my English friend told me, in a moment of rare openness, only strengthened the feeling. In the closed, expatriate, cocktail circuits of Kolkata, even as the Sahibs, both brown and white, watched regretfully the sun set on the British Empire, India was referred to as the land of "spit, shit and snot". Everything seemed to conspire to make the Indian feel small. Even *Pather Panchali*, so to say, tugged at your heartstrings and diminished you. It put on show the despair of Indian poverty which is only half the story. It took Mother Teresa to point out the other and more important half. When Muggeridge asked her the inevitable question on India's poverty, she responded without hesitation: "In India, there is no poverty of the spirit." For the first time in over twenty years the Indian tri-colour unfurled in my heart, and flew full-mast.

It is this very same current of spirituality that bears forward in its powerful flow the traditions of Indian classical music, or dance and theatre, for that matter. In our performing arts, spirituality is not an option left to chance and individual choice. It is formally worked into the learning process and instilled into students by their gurus. It is part of their training. They are never allowed to overlook or forget it. They are taught to delve inwards and transcend even their own musical abilities.

A typical performance demonstrates this. The musician closes his eyes, centres himself and humming, invites the spirit to enter. Then enunciating, phrasing, with and between the notes, exploring them, he pleads, implores and finally surrenders, allowing the spirit of music to take over. It is an act of *bhakti*, devotion, an erasing of the ego. Singer and song have become one and undifferentiated. He is in touch with the very source of his being. At the same time, reaching out, he taps the same source in the listener who receives the experience and recreates it. Such is the ideal performance and every musician worth the name, strains after it.

In the Indian metaphysical tradition, creation is linked to sound, *nada*—the first hum that spun the universe into being from the formless substratum of Non-being, from the Unmanifest into the Manifest. Sound, which is the basis of music, formulates into the mystic syllable Om, referred to as *Brahma nada*, which then articulates as Vak word and speech, the currency of poetry and song.

Music is, therefore, meditation. Its daily practice is prayer and invocation, and its periodic display or performance an offering to the source of Being itself, the *hridayi akasha*, the space within the heart of each one, infinitesimal and infinite at the same time. It is this hidden enclave that holds in safe-keeping the treasure that, throughout their lives on earth all Indians hunt for— *mukti*, release. The gifted artist hunts with single-minded fervour. It is his responsibility to seek, and equally his responsibility to share. That is the only justification for the practice and performance of music as the Indian sees it. It is not entertainment. Its object is not to while away time, or to merely please. Its aim is to share a spiritual journey.

Music is also *leela*, sport, in a philosophical sense, with *prana*, life-breath. It is virtually *pranayama*, breath control, an established yogic practice. Purifying sound, filtering it through the *vishuddhi chakra* situated in the throat, directing it painstakingly with and between the notes, the musician is going through the paces of *pranayama*. He is literally handling and giving shape to the stuff of life.

The insights and perceptions of sages and seers were endorsed by religion. Dance and music were given the temple for a setting. Ustad Aminuddin Dagar, exponent of the Dhrupad school of music, once said to me when I remarked on the lack of respect for musicians in contemporary audiences: "What respect? In our tradition the musician did not face an audience or perform for it. He faced the sanctum and sought neither the respect nor the approval of the gathering. He performed for the deity, and they experienced with him the grace of God." I would like to quote an example or two from my own experience. M.S. Subbulakshmi's early music was made for the cinema. The film Meera brought her into the limelight in the forties. It was a beautiful depiction of *bhakti*, but it was still only a depiction. Her early classical performances were models of grace and elegance—immaculate stage presence, perfect musical manners and a honey-sweet voice. Over the years, the manners, the voice, the craft, the striking beauty of her presence seemed to matter less and less. Every performance had been internalised and was an exercise in sheer meditation. When last I heard her nothing, not even her own music, stood between her and deep spiritual communion. On me, as on many in that audience, she cast, without intending to, the spell of true yoga—accord with oneself.

Pandit Bhimsen Joshi, in an interview with All India Radio, Lucknow, was asked about the devotional and spiritual turn that his music was taking. The maestro answered quite simply: "Isn't it inevitable?" His early performances were like wrestling matches with the demons of sound within him. There was a frenzy, a desperation in each spectacular struggle as he grappled with notes and phrases, wringing every drop of music out of them. And then the full, ripe roundness of his music set in. It swelled and flowed over his audiences like a tidal wave of benediction. It was the same with M.D. Ramanathan. He would roar and race his way through a performance; with the passing of years, musical maturity and the spirit took over. Slow and unhurried, he trod the path of great music, a pilgrim grounded in faith and reaching for salvation.

I have lived to see musicians bargain for exorbitant fees, demand fancy sound systems which they insist on fine-tuning themselves, while audiences wait restlessly for the performance to begin. I have seen some indulge in calculated displays of the artistic temperament, others play to the gallery for effect and even mock the public. But the best of them, thanks to the continuing Indian tradition, settle down thereafter to the serious business of music, transporting themselves and their listeners to the heady realms of spiritual exaltation. Any brush with Indian classical music leaves one in no doubt about its true nature—it is the spirit that sings, and will continue to sing in India.

Saraswati, Goddess of Learning and Music

For song and meaning to meet in good measure
for consonance apt, that alchemy fine
glance my way, goddess and grant me your boon
source of all learning, Saraswati
be the white swan that can rid milk of water
take the poetry and song that your faithfuls here
offer...
rid it of dross, so it's nectar-like, clear
take what is good, and let the rest be.

— Kumaraguruparar